George R. Collins

Visionary Drawings of Architecture and Planning
20th Century through the 1960s

The Drawing Center
137 Greene Street
New York, New York 10012

Developed for Travel and
Circulated by the Smithsonian
Institution Traveling
Exhibition Service (SITES)

1979

The MIT Press
Cambridge, Massachusetts, and London, England

First MIT Press edition 1979

Second printing, 1980

Printed in the United States of America

*A generous grant supporting this exhibition is contributed by the
New York Council for the Humanities, a state program of the
National Endowment for the Humanities. This project and The
Drawing Center are made possible in part with public funds
provided by the New York State Council on the Arts.*

*Directors: Edward H. Tuck, Chairman; Martha Beck; George R.
Collins; Colin Eisler; John B. Hightower; Stephen J. Hoffman;
Douglas Newton; Elizabeth Vagliano.*

Library of Congress catalog card number: 78–78218
ISBN 0–262–03070–5

The Drawing Center

The Drawing Center, founded by Martha Beck less than two years ago, seeks through exhibition and education to express the quality and diversity of drawing as a major art form. A small institution (albeit the only one with its objectives in this country), the Center will continue to respond quickly and flexibly to artistic opportunities while maintaining the high curatorial and educational standards of much larger institutions. The generous physical space at The Drawing Center enables the showing of works there which could not be shown in many museums.

The drawings of Antonio Gaudí exhibited in the Spring of last year helped set a pattern for the Center's approach—to exploit fully the possibilities created by the presentation of a great artist's work. The exhibition (a first showing of Gaudí drawings outside Spain and the largest showing ever) included full text panels and pictures of the completed buildings represented; it was accompanied by a catalogue with an important essay on the architect by Professor George R. Collins and a series of seven lectures, colloquia, and films on Gaudí work. Students and staff were at the Center every day to provide information to the public.

Through other major exhibitions of established artists (of which there have now been six), the Center has attracted an unusual audience for the drawings of younger, lesser known artists in its group shows (of which there have been five) which are themselves assembled largely as a result of the viewing program. 2,500 artists have shown their work to the Center since the inception of the program, the work of 50 has been exhibited in our group shows and 26 artists have now sold their first drawings. (As a nonprofit organization, the Center has no financial interest in these sales.)

The critical reception given the Center's work to date has been outstanding. With the presentation of this exhibition which, thanks to the Smithsonian Institution Traveling Exhibition Service, will journey for two years to more than 15 cities, The Drawing Center takes another step toward the fulfillment of its objectives.

We take this occasion to thank those whose financial support makes us cautiously confident of a useful future.

For the Board of Directors

Edward H. Tuck
Chairman

Acknowledgments

The Drawing Center takes great pleasure in presenting this exhibition, "Visionary Drawings of Architecture and Planning," directed by George R. Collins, Professor of Art History at Columbia University. Professor Collins' scholarship, enthusiasm, and charm have endowed this exhibition and catalogue with a special value. We are deeply indebted and grateful to him.

We should like particularly to thank:
Victoria Newhouse, President of the Architectural History Foundation, who generously donated the production of the catalogue and kindly provided indispensable assistance with its publication. Equal thanks are due her colleague, Julianne Griffin, for her expert aid.

Massimo Vignelli, who generously donated the design of the catalogue and announcements.

The architects, museums, and collectors who have lent to the exhibition, for their enthusiastic willingness to share their works and knowledge; and among them particularly the Busch-Reisinger Museum, Harvard University; Professor Adolf K. Placzek, Avery Librarian, Columbia University; André Emmerich Gallery; Ronald Feldman Fine Arts; Medard Gabel, The Buckminster Fuller Archive; Howard Gilman, Chairman, Gilman Paper Co.; to Natalie Moody and Pierre Apraxine, Curator, Gilman Paper Collection; Arthur Drexler, Director, Architecture and Design, Museum of Modern Art; Ludwig Glaeser, Curator, Mies van der Rohe Archive, Museum of Modern Art; University of Oregon, Library of Architecture and Allied Arts Branch; Department of Architecture, University of Pennsylvania; and the Department of Special Collections, Research Library, University of California, Los Angeles.

Dr. Laura Tampieri of the Italian Cultural Institute; Professor Marco Miele, Director, Italian Cultural Institute; Francesco Passanti; André Gadaud, Cultural Counselor, Permanent Representative in the United States of French Universities; and Claire Mahot, French Cultural Services, for their extraordinary friendship and help.

The architects and architectural historians who contributed catalogue entries and thereby greatly enriched this catalogue.

Christine Chamberlain Dow of the National Endowment for the Arts, whose encouragement was an incentive to begin work on this exhibition; Carol Groneman, Executive Director, and Martin Beller, Research Associate, the New York Council for the Humanities, who allowed us to realize fully our plan; and to Constance Eiseman, Lucy Kostelanetz, James Runish, Joan Rosenbaum, and Darrell Schulze of the New York State Council on the Arts for their encouragement and aid.

Dennis A. Gould, Director, Smithsonian Institution Traveling Exhibition Service; Quinton Hallett, Exhibition Coordinator; Antonio Diez, Administrative Officer, for their help in preparing the two-year tour of the exhibition throughout the United States under the auspices of SITES.

Michael Iovenko, who has kindly and generously donated his legal services.

Huntington T. Block for his concerned attention to our security and insurance.

I wish personally to thank:
Edward H. Tuck, who as chairman of the board has made The Drawing Center the success it is.

Colin T. Eisler, Robert Lehman Professor of Fine Arts, Institute of Fine Arts, New York University, the first member of the board and an invaluable supporter and friend.

We are proud to present this exhibition; its success is due to a group effort. Major contributions to this effort were made by Ada V. Ciniglio, Director of Development, and Marie Therese Keller, Assistant Curator and Registrar of The Drawing Center.

Since January 15, 1977, when The Drawing Center opened, it has been lucky enough to gather a large group of friends who have generously donated a wealth of expertise. I thank them all.

Martha Beck
Director

Foreword

by

George R. Collins

This exhibition came about as a result of my general interest as an art historian in the theory of modern architecture and planning. For a number of years I have applied myself to visionary and utopian considerations in this matter, writing the Introduction to the book *Unbuilt America* in 1976 and attempting to conclude my own book on Visionary Planning during the academic year 1976–77 while on a Rockefeller Foundation Humanities Fellowship. It seemed to me that a study of the art produced by visionaries—i.e., drawings—might be the proper interest of an art historian. Hence the exhibition.

What I had not counted on was the fact that the drawings were to be as illusory and fugitive as the visions themselves. Many were apparently retained or discarded by publishers who printed them and did not return them to the designer; often the artists themselves had no idea where the drawings might be. I found one lining a tube in which others had been packed and shipped. In general it can be said that they have not been treasured, although I think that many may be as important as built buildings and they do run the gamut of architectural drawing types, so that this exhibit, although not originally intended as such, stands as an almost complete demonstration of what architectural drawings are.

I think that this is the first exhibition of a group of visionaries that limits itself exclusively to their original drawings. Because most architectural drawings and records tend to be neglected and lost, we have chosen to present the works here exhibited as far as possible *as is*, that is to say, as found—with the mold, paper degeneration, coffee stains, and creases of the hard or abandoned life they have led. It is hoped that if the public finds them attractive as records and as works of art, it may assist us in our present efforts to find and restore these documents.[1]

It may be because there are usually no patrons for visionary projects that the drawings disappear. In much architectural practice, the office is cleaned out periodically (Kenzo Tange reports that he never keeps drawings), but a drawing is sometimes saved because it is in the hands of the patron, even if the structure was never built. If the drawing served for some utopian article in a periodical, it probably went the way of authors' photographs, often not returned or recovered. Of course, many visionary drawings were not meant to be published or produced for a public, but instead were the inner thoughts or contemplation of the person who sketched them; these may be neglected later or outgrown, stored away if at all in no place in particular. Certainly few people who had to move about as much as Andrew Weininger would have managed to keep in sight their own student drawings—thereby documenting for us a critical point in the history of the Bauhaus *(fig. 59)*.

My search was, in many cases, so difficult that certain relevant movements are not at all represented in the exhibition. For instance, in spite of the advice and assistance of Anatole Kopp from Paris, S. Frederick Starr from Washington, D.C., and Rem Koolhaas from London, we were unable to procure any drawings of the exciting Soviet projects of the 1920s/1930s which do indeed exist but could not be obtained in the time I had allotted myself for preparation of the exhibition. The de Stijl movement of the 1920s is represented only by its reflection in the aforementioned Bauhaus student drawings, and there are loopholes in the visionary movements of the 1960s, not for any lack of interest on my part but only because I could not cover everything. Time also militated against my locating a missing visionary project of Walter Gropius despite the active help of his widow, and we simply could not pry loose the only surviving drawings by Tony Garnier for his *cité industrielle*.

It should be noted that this catalogue deals not only with drawings (it is not expected that architects, planners, and engineers are necessarily great graphic artists) but with the subject of the visionary in general: what are the various aspects of it and in what order roughly did the visionaries appear in our century? Nor is this a complete catalogue raisonné of twentieth-century visionary drawings, for the reasons mentioned above. We do hope, however, that we have been truly representative of both the types of projects and the techniques of drawing and rendering. I have also attempted to achieve a certain catholicity of taste by inviting colleagues, students, and other friends to join in writing on those drawings or individuals in which they have an interest. In all such cases the author's name appears at the conclusion of the catalogue entry. If I have supplied part of such an entry it is so indicated with my initials, "G.R.C." I am responsible for the unsigned entries.

Further to put this material in perspective—it dates from c. 1900 to c. 1970, that is to say, it is a retrospective exhibition—there is a corollary presentation of slides of visionary drawings of former times such as the medieval apocalyptic City of God, Leonardo da Vinci's multilevel Renaissance town, Piranesi's fantasies, and the like, with a taped commentary by myself on the prior history of the visionary.

And I hope that readers of this catalogue will forgive me if I have not sounded the usual warnings about visionary projects. That they are at times formalistic, overgeneralized, authoritarian, and sociologically simplistic is obvious; hopefully the imagination of most of the designers and the consummate artistry of some of them will outweigh such ethical reservations.

This exhibition could never have been mounted nor the catalogue printed without the aid of many persons.

I am deeply indebted to the following, who wrote catalogue entries for me, carefully adhering to the limits that were set for each biography and drawing: Thomas Anderson (2), Reyner Banham, Rosemarie Haag Bletter (2), Richard Cleary (4), Christiane C. Collins (2), Mary D. Edwards, Janet Kaplan, Reginald Malcolmson, Peter Marangoni, Peter McCleary, Eugene Santomasso, Vincent Scully, Janet White (2), and Carol Willis (3). The following individuals assisted me by writing about their own work: Raimund Abraham, Reginald Malcolmson, Shoji Sadao, Mario G. Salvadori, Friedrich St. Florian, Anne Griswold Tyng, Michael Webb, and Andrew Weininger.

Many others tendered me aid. The Japanese architects Arato Isozaki, Kiyonori Kikutake, and Kisho Kurokawa put into my hands to choose from on my visit to Tokyo in January 1978 *all* of the drawings that they have left from the 1960s, and Fumihiko Maki (who had none left) was also especially helpful. For assistance with the work of specific individuals I am indebted to many: *Ferriss*, Ann Ferriss Harris (his niece), Ferdinand Eiseman, and Carol Willis; *Fuller*, Edgar J. Applewhite, Medard Gabel, Shoji Sadao, and Buckminster Fuller himself; *Gropius*, Charles Haxthausen, Karen Davidson, James M. Fitch, and Ise Gropius; *Hablik,* Eugene

Santomasso and Susanne Klingeberg-Hablik (his daughter); *Kahn*, Vincent Scully, Anne Griswold Tyng; *Lamb*, Barea Lamb Seeley (his granddaughter); *Kiesler*, James Yohe, Bayat Keerl, André Emmerich, and Mrs. Kiesler; *Le Corbusier*, Jerzy W. Soltan, Kenneth A. Smith, Geysa Sarkany, Jr., and Neil Robert Berzak; *Mendelsohn*, Ricardo Castro, Marion D. Ross, and Mrs. Mendelsohn; *Mies van der Rohe*, Ludwig Glaeser, Philip Johnson, Reginald Malcolmson, Paul Thomas, A. James Speyer, George Danforth, Alfred Swenson, and Pao-Chi Chang; *Neutra*, Thomas S. Hines and Mrs. Neutra; *Sant'Elia*, Francesco Passanti, Dennis Doordan, Reyner Banham, Consuelo Accetti, Marco Miele, Laura Neagli, and Bruno Zevi; *Parent*, Edgar Kaufmann, jr.; *Frank Lloyd Wright*, Philip I. Danzig, Mrs. Irwin Elkus Auerbach, and David T. Henken; *Lloyd Wright*, his son Eric; other *German Expressionists*, H.H. Waechter, O.M. Ungers, Eberhard Roters, Joachim v. Rosenberg, Margaret Scharoun, Achim Wendschuh, and Rosemarie Haag Bletter.

Herbert H. Stevens, Jr., Konrad Wachsmann, and Amancio Williams were particularly helpful in giving me information about their own work.

The exhibition might never have been thought of and certainly would not have come about but for the staff of The Drawing Center, especially Martha Beck, James Hoekema, Ada V. Ciniglio, and my indefatigable friend Marie Therese Keller. Likewise this catalogue would never have appeared, as it did in record time despite my own latenesses, if it were not for the remarkable know-how of Victoria Newhouse and Julianne Griffin of the Architectural History Foundation, Inc., and Massimo Vignelli, the designer—all of them volunteers like myself in this enterprise.

I owe much to our photographers, Mary Ellen Keane, Phil Smith, and Dan Russell, and my two typists, Paula Spilner and Sally Umberger, as well as the office staff of the Department of Art History and Archaeology at Columbia, in particular Helene A. Farrow, our administrative officer.

But ultimately my greatest appreciation goes to the Rockefeller Foundation, which gave me a year to think, and to the several individuals who then helped me in the process of thinking about drawings: Michael Hollander, Reginald Malcolmson, Adolf K. Placzek, Phyllis Braff, Robert Cleary, Carol Willis, and Christiane C. Collins.

To close I can do no better than quote from my friend Reginald Malcolmson who wrote in the catalogue of his own visionary exhibition:

"Projects point the way towards the future. They are signposts indicating the direction towards future possible worlds . . . .

"The making of projects is a continuum—they are initiated, undergo critical analysis, modification, and refinement so that, in a sense, they never reach finality—not merely because they remain unbuilt, but because they tend to remain work in progress . . . ." [2]

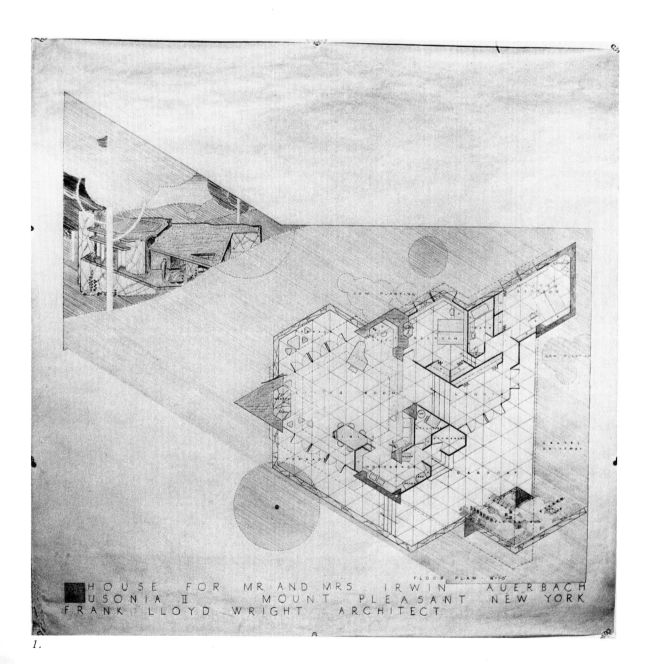

HOUSE FOR MR AND MRS IRWIN AUERBACH
USONIA II MOUNT PLEASANT NEW YORK
FRANK LLOYD WRIGHT ARCHITECT

1.

Introduction

by George R. Collins

My intention is to discuss the nature of the visionary, what the visionary has contributed in our century, and just what drawings of this kind—paper architecture—are and can be. The purpose of the exhibition is to demonstrate the wide range that comes under the heading of "visionary" and how in our century many major movements can perhaps be understood better in terms of the drawings and aspirations of their various members than through their built structures in the realization of which their precepts may have been altered.

I

The nature of the visionary in architecture, planning, and engineering is such that it defies exact definition.[3]

In general the visionary represents a theoretical, speculative, or even imaginary statement or position that is likely to be considerably ahead of its time and may not even be intended to be carried out. The term "visionary" is not, however, synonymous with "unbuilt" and cannot be restricted to projects that are not or cannot be put into effect as the *Oxford English Dictionary* suggests.

That a number of visionary drawings exhibited here were produced with specific places in mind such as New York City, Tokyo, Los Angeles, or the airplane carrier *Enterprise,* does not necessarily reduce their concept to the status of "unbuilt" but simply supplies certain conditions to be taken into account, an appropriateness of the suggested solution, or a familiarity to the viewer: the concept may still be quite fanciful and even impractical in nature. Furthermore a visionary project may be a specific building type such as a bridge, a church, a house, a station, or a theater. For instance, we are exhibiting drawings by Frank Lloyd Wright for a particular house for a Usonian community that could well have been built *(fig. 1),* but the fact that the drawing was labelled "Usonia II" gives it so many Wrightian overtones of a utopian and socially theoretical character that it partakes of the poetic in architecture, i.e., is visionary. So the visionary can also be sensed in built structures—not only grandiloquent ones like the Egyptian pyramids, the Eiffel Tower, and the Empire State Building, but also in the more modest or even fragmentary works of an intensely symbolic designer, like Antonio Gaudí.

Sometimes a model vision is not really intended to be built at the time—like Ludwig Mies van der Rohe's Glass Tower *(fig. 81)*—but is later executed more or less as projected; today our advanced technology makes possible almost anything, even the most daring dreams. On the other hand a visionary scheme may bear only a corollary or abstract relation to physical actuality and be rather a statement of spiritual or intellectual commitment or fantasy on the part of the designer.

There are a number of terms that are often employed, as we do here, as synonyms for or as aspects of the visionary. We have already used the expressions "imaginary," "fantasy," and "speculative," which are obvious in their meaning if not precise. Another such related term is "futurist," especially in our century when the idea of human progress has tended to hold sway. Many visionary projects are futurist in the sense that they are based on a passage of time until the technological or social conditions arrive that would make the project attainable. The visionary can then be prophetic in an Old Testament sense; and it matters not whether it comes about in one's own lifetime since one can still conduct oneself in accordance with it. Does it thereby attain a transcendental reality—more real than we ourselves are? Dean Inge wrote, "Ecstasy or vision begins when thought ceases, to our consciousness, to proceed from ourselves."[4]

Technology has been much involved in 20th-century visionary thinking just as social issues were in that of the 19th century. Charles Beard, in his Introduction to J.B. Bury's *The Idea of Progress* (1932 edit.), called technology "the supreme instrument of modern progress" and "a subjective force of high tension." As he says—and as we can comprehend from gazing at the drawings of Richard Neutra, Buckminster Fuller, Kiyonori Kikutake, or Paolo Soleri—"it embraces within its scope great constellations of ideas, some explored to apparent limits and others in the form of posed problems and emergent issues dimly understood." Technological visionaries may concern themselves with ultimate physical forces, as did Hugh Ferriss, or with systems (that is, a concern with the process that engenders form) as does Anne Tyng.

The tendency to systematize, or to sub-optimize, one or another aspect of function has long been apparent in city

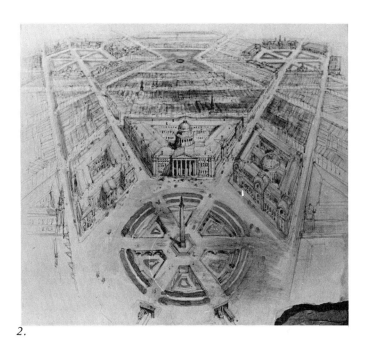

2.

3.

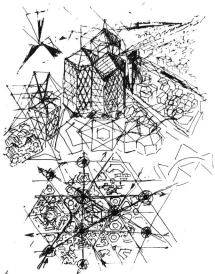

4.

plans of what are called the "ideal" type. Ideal planning as a vision implies the search for a better society by means of special, faultless, a-priori physical arrangements; the ideal city would be a city of physical perfection, and visionary planners have invariably sought just that. The ideal plan has often been presented in schematic, abstract form, if only for reasons of graphic clarity, and the form if geometric can take on a certain perfection in itself. In the Renaissance, for instance, the various ideal layouts—even when incorporating the presumably practical matters of protection from attack— give the effect of pure *Formspiel*. In our century the aesthetics of the French Beaux Arts and American City Beautiful echoed these values, as seen in Charles Lamb's Model City *(figs. 2, 3)*. Geometric modules also underlie the architectural structures of many designers, e.g., Robert Le Ricolais *(fig. 4)* and Frank Lloyd Wright *(fig. 97)*, although we would not use the adjective "ideal" to designate their works in the way we do for a geometrically arranged town plan.

For the planner there are, of course, ideals other than the geometric, but some prime geometrical configurations tend to become "models" and their subsequent use bespeaks certain underlying concepts as would a literary quotation, say from Shakespeare. Thus the fact that the ideal plan of a learned designer like James Silk Buckingham in 1849 was patently based on prior plans by Dürer of the early 16th century, Schickhardt of the late 16th century, and Andreae of the early 17th century does not denote plagiarism but rather loads Buckingham's plan with historical visionary ideas, much as the "post-modernist" architects of today seek to achieve meaning in their buildings by symbolic references in their designs. Likewise, in visionary *architectural* schemas a reliance on Platonic geometry of ancient times, e.g., in the projects of Wenzel Hablik *(fig. 5)*, presumably contributes an almost divine essence to the concept and requires a certain iconographic knowledge to unravel its meanings.

In planning, certain models like the gridiron plan are quite natural, easily reproducible, and are simply useful for certain functions, but carry no particular meaning. Although the architect, planner, or engineer is usually supported financially by an individual or an institution, most visionary projects, as opposed to "real" projects, tend not to have a specific patron or user. For this reason they tend to be generalized in intent, i.e., to serve as a model; the model, of course, may be developed eventually with great specificity.

5.

6. *Hans Scharoun, Untitled Drawing, 1919.* No. 92.
7. *Paolo Soleri, The Six Suns, 1960 (detail).* No. 96.
8. *Hugh Ferriss, The Lure of the City, c. 1925.* No. 8.
9. *Hablik, A Colony-in-the-Air, 1908.* No. 22.

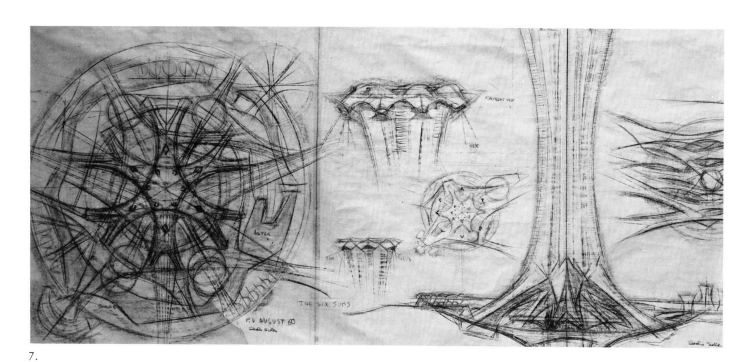

7.

6.

8.

The term "utopian," the use of which is restricted mainly to planning, refers rather to proposed social arrangements than to the physical form of the plan or layout. However utopians have frequently been formalists and have postulated geometrically abstract patterns for their settlements. As an idea, "utopia" is ancient, but the term itself originated with Sir Thomas More c. 1516: *topos* (place) plus the punning prefix *eu* (good) and/or *ou* (not), to wit, "good place nowhere."

Utopias have stemmed from discontent with existing society, and they aim to improve it (and the nature of man) to the point of perfection by altering his associations and circumstances—namely by social planning. The desired social change, if it comes about, may or may not be triggered by or be a function of the physical structure of the utopia. Utopias were characteristic of the 19th century; visionaries in our century have tended to be more technological, aesthetic, poetic, futuristic in their designing than socially reformist. Exceptions to this would be Tony Garnier (whose drawings we have been unable to obtain), the German Expressionists *(fig. 6),* Frank Lloyd Wright *(fig. 1),* and Paolo Soleri *(fig. 7).*

There remains another sort of vision, the "cosmological," that is also not as characteristic of our century. Cosmological procedures were adopted since ancient times in order to situate a plan or an edifice in harmony with the larger extra-terrestrial universe. In contrast with utopia, cosmology attempted to adjust man to his inherited environment by means of divinatory practices—magic. If they exist at all, cosmological planning and building in our century take on utilitarian and technological qualities as in the designs for exploring and inhabiting outer space. There is a sense of direct cosmic wonder in certain renderings by Hugh Ferriss *(fig. 8),* and the drawings of the German Expressionists sometimes deal with interplanetary inventions *(fig. 9),* but nothing in the present exhibition can be said to derive from divinatory practices unless it be Soleri's *Six Suns (fig. 7).* Admittedly science fiction and its illustrations are to a certain extent part of the age-old tradition of imaginary cosmology; we have, however, avoided science fiction in our exhibition in part because its *art* is almost invariably second-hand —by artists independent of the authors—and is of the character of "magazine graphics" discussed below.

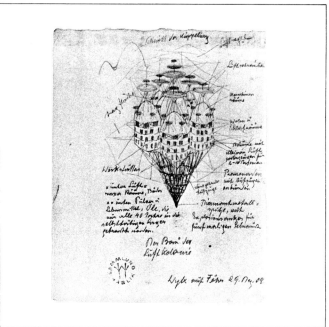

9.

Thus the visionary encompasses a wide range of both concept-type and drawing-character. It may be thought of as a stage in arriving at something or the projection of situations quite beyond our reach. It can reside, therefore, in a precise and highly detailed drawing or in the vaguest, most bizarre sketch or doodle. It may be abstract and diagrammatic in drawn form in order to suggest a process or system of a mechanistic sort, or rather to imply that it is of a higher, cosmic order. It may be impressionist, expressionist, or tightly dogmatic in style—either literally symbolic or ambiguous in content. It may delineate a general a-priori model for almost universal use, or it may be a matter of purely personal fantasy, even playful or mocking. The visionary may be seen as a critique of current practice rather than as a suggestion of future forms. Whether the adjective "real" or "universal" should be used for the visionary I leave to the viewer of this exhibition. It should be understood that "visionary" is what an outsider, a third party, calls projects which the designer may consider to be of the ultimate reality and practicality. In fact, it might be said about architecture and planning that what is called "visionary" is not of the future but the natural realization of today's higher aspirations, and what is actually being built today is the visionary of yesterday.

II

The types of visionary projects that have appeared in the 20th century can be categorized by either their programmes—viz. functional character—or, more metaphorically, by what inspired them.

As regards the first kind of typology, we are concerned, of course, with ideas about buildings, technical structures, and town planning. Many designers, especially in the first half of our century, tended to continue the interests of their predecessors in the 19th century: tall edifices, cult buildings, houses and housing, public buildings, buildings for spectacles, transportation stations, bridges, and structural frames. In the field of planning there are suggestions for new towns and cities, for regions—especially decentralized planning like the linear city—and methods for the recycling of older cities. There are also projects of pure fantasy. In the late 1950s and the 1960s a variety of new proposals appear, reflecting the "sputnik" mentality of that decade. Ideas that

were rare earlier (Cf. *fig. 9*) or were only to be found in science fiction stories take on a new realism, and we find serious suggestions for the megastructure with capsule and plug-in elements; container cities providing artificial environments; marine projects on piles, floating, or submarine (operating either with surface pressure or ambient pressure); subterranean buildings and settlements on earth, or on the heavenly bodies, that do not derive from post World War II fear of atomic attack; and, finally, a whole range of extraterrestrial architecture and planning either put into orbit from the earth, constructed in space, or built on celestial bodies.

Other methods have been tried to type modern visionary projects, notably on the occasion of the Exhibition of Visionary Architecture at New York's Museum of Modern Art in 1960 and in the publication of Conrads and Sperlich's *Phantastische Architektur* that same year. Arthur Drexler of the Museum of Modern Art distinguished three basic classes of the visionary in his exhibition: 1) the goal at the end of a journey, for example the image of a mountain; 2) the experience of the road itself, of which bridge structures are a clear instance; and 3) forms that seem to confine or intensify emotional experience, such as those derived from geometry. Conrads and Sperlich listed a dozen categories, including the fantastic framework, the fascination with transparency, the sheltering cave, *Formspiel*, hovering architecture, utopias, futurism, and the obsession with height. Such figurative categories as these and those of the Modern Museum have the advantage of not just classifying visionary projects, but actually giving a sensation of their purpose and artistry.

III

Another manner of viewing and classifying visionary ideas in our century is the chronological one, determining the sequence in which individuals emerged and movements developed. As might be expected, the history of the visionary is marked by independent thinkers on the one hand and by cohesive, almost doctrinaire, schools of thought on the other.

One would normally start with Tony Garnier (1869–1948) whose *cité industrielle*—evolved while he was on a Prix de Rome in Italy in the opening years of the century—set the stage for much visionary planning and architecture in

subsequent decades. Generally Fourierist in concept, it
continued the 19th-century tradition of utopian settlements;
but designed as it was for heavy industry, powered by clean
water-generated electricity, and constructed in poured
concrete, it was to be an inspiration to the technological
fervor of 20th-century visionaries. Unfortunately, none of
Garnier's drawings for his first project of 1901–04 seem to
have survived, and the later aerial perspectives that he did for
his 1917 publication of the *cité industrielle* were declared to be
in too fragile a condition to travel to our exhibition.

Much less known, but of similar extraction in the sense that
his American City Beautiful aesthetic shares much of the
same monumentality of effect, achieved by softening
classicistic modern buildings with rich vegetation, is the
American artist-planner Charles R. Lamb (1860–1942).
Lamb's attention was on improving the metropolis as it
existed, not setting out new towns, but his suggested
revisions are sweeping in that they argue for hexagonal block
and city layouts on the one hand and streets high on
skyscrapers on the other—both of them concepts to be
popular with visionaries down to the present *(fig. 10).*

10.

Another visionary of these years, again French and out of the
Beaux Arts tradition, was Eugene Hénard (1849–1923).
Considering himself a successor to Baron Haussmann,
Hénard applied himself to metropolitan reform, especially in
Paris—sometimes in quite visionary ways such as his
multi-level streets and the re-use of the Champs de Mars as an
airport, as well as his invention of full-speed urban traffic
interchanges. Again, sadly, none of the drawings for his
projects as published in fascicules between 1903–09 appear
to have survived. The projects were influential, however,
because of his participation in international congresses, and
they may well have affected Sant'Elia and Le Corbusier,
among others.

Radical decentralists also were to be found among early
20th-century planners, again stemming in part from late
19th-century ideas. An example of this is the inventor Edgar
Chambless (1871–1936) with his Roadtown *(fig. 11),* a
continuous house with rapid rail transport under it, to be
constructed of poured concrete on the Edison patent.
Sounding very technocratic and actually a prototype of the
megastructures of the 1960s which were supposed to be
self-extending by means of their built-in transport and

11.

12. *Antonio Sant'Elia, Città Nuova, 1914.* No. 90.
13. *Hermann Finsterlin, Concert Hall.* No. 11.
14. *Walter Gropius, Total Theater, 1926.* No. 20.

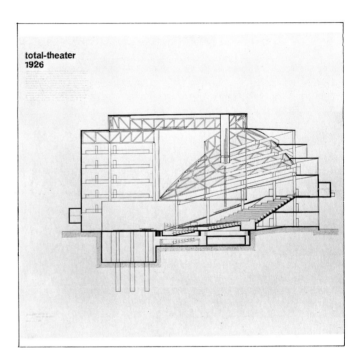

total-theater
1926

14.

12.

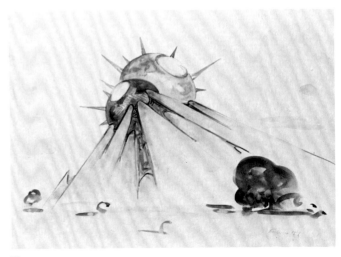

13.

construction processes, Roadtown was really agrarian, its ultimate purpose being to get its residents into easy contact with the countryside. Each could then garden or farm on his own acre close by the continuous concrete band whose flat roof also served as a covered promenade and provided communal services. Unfortunately, the original renderings for Chambless's book, articles, and broadsides—presumably not done by him anyway—are not to be found.

It is an easy step from Hénard and Chambless to the visions of Italian Futurism of the 'teens, represented architecturally by the drawings of Antonio Sant'Elia (1888–1916), a short-lived and almost entirely "paper" architect who, whether or not he so intended, is taken as the physical manifestation of that movement's thoughts about building and planning *(fig. 12).* It is an intensely metropolitan vision with an exaggeration of all the urban and industrial power and zip of that day. His images are intensely, but not thoroughly, urban because those of Sant'Elia's projects that include more than a single structure seem to deal only with a nexus of back-and-forth horizontal movement and up-and-down constructed vertical transport. He emphasized the possibility of tightly scheduled intersecting movements, but passengers do not appear in his perspectives as we see the people-movement in contemporary Futurist paintings of the city. How immediately influential Sant'Elia was in the international spread of Futurist ideology via Marinetti and others is not clear, but he does seem to be the forerunner of many visionary projects (and even film scenarios) of the 1920s—those of Le Corbusier, Neutra, Ferriss, Hilberseimer, and the Soviets included.

At the end of the war—in which Sant'Elia perished—the visionary flowered in Germany in a burst of architectural expressionism that derived, ambiguously, from both the optimism and the despair that marked the years 1918–23. I think it could be maintained that, although the movement was composed largely of architects, whose projects ranged from monuments and single buildings to vast terrestrial and superterrestrial planning, the thrust was primarily a literary one, as if the drawings (which are often virtually paintings) were meant to be illustrations of social, political, or literary manifestoes. It is not that they are so literal—most are highly abstract—but they seem to bear a message, and often the message is furthered by staccato calligraphic phrases spattered about the edges of the drawings. Helmsman of the

group was, of course, Bruno Taut, but the original drawings for his Expressionist graphics, if they still existed, disappeared when his office archive in Berlin burned during World War II. We have on exhibition comparable works by Wenzel Hablik (1881–1934) *(figs. 5, 9, 68),* Hermann Finsterlin (1887–1974) *(figs. 13, 64),* and Hans Scharoun (1893–1972) *(figs. 6, 87)* which illustrate the major tendencies of the movement. More simply architectural, of course, and to be extremely influential for many decades to come, are the renderings by Ludwig Mies van der Rohe (1887–1969) of those years—outstanding examples of that "never-built" in architecture which has exerted as much or more influence on the development and talk about architecture (they are pictured in every textbook) than any "real," built structure *(fig. 81).*

All four of the so-called "Great Makers of Modern Architecture"—Wright, Gropius, Mies, Le Corbusier— have been, at one time or another and in one way or another, visionaries. Of Mies van der Rohe we show a project of the Expressionist period, of Gropius a Bauhaus project, but of Wright a project from later in his career when he had become concerned with certain social ideas for which he used the terms Usonia and Usonian. Le Corbusier was always a utopian of sorts, as Robert Fishman has made clear in his *Urban Utopias in the Twentieth Century,* and we show sketches from the 1930s and from the twilight of his career on occasions when he, like Eric Mendelsohn, would draw as he lectured.

The Bauhaus was intended as, or at least came to be, a way of life as well as an instructional operation, and it would appear that one of its integral activities was that of drama, performance, dance, and play. So it is not surprising that its director, with the cooperation of Erwin Piscator, worked out an ideal, universal theater *(fig. 14).* For some reason the theater is a favorite design project of the visionaries— presumably for the opportunity it affords for them to evoke physically a visionary world. A Bauhaus student, Andrew Weininger, also designed one, as did the Soviets at the time, and we have on exhibition theaters by Kiesler, Williams, and Malcolmson.

Actually, Soviet Russia, one of the major areas in which the modern movement developed in the 1920s, produced the most spectacular visionary projects, perhaps because of early Soviet identification of the architectural with the social-political revolution—"transformation of the way of life" as they called it. We have been unable, despite considerable effort, to obtain original drawings that correspond to the projects of the Vesnin brothers, Moisei Ginzburg, Ivan Leonidov, Konstantin Melnikov, Iakov Chernikov (who published a book, *Architectural Fantasies*, in 1933) or to the famous linear layout of N.A. Miliutin for the Stalingrad area that has become almost a logo of assembly-line production planning.

During almost these same years, 1923–35, the Viennese-American architect Richard Neutra (1892–1970) first worked over his carefully detailed Rush City Reformed *(fig. 15)*. It is a linear city reflecting the speed of Sant'Elia's Futurism, but laid out flat and spreading, acknowledging for perhaps the first time in visionary planning the importance of the automobile, on which the plan is predicated. The interest of the drawings for this project is that they reveal the complexity of the research carried out in order to accommodate a wide spectrum of types of people and activities in modern society and not simply the technology of interchanges for fast-moving streams of traffic as we frequently see Rush City presented. Neutra believed that we can survive through design, sensitive design. While it is true that his layout did tend to put into their own zones differentiated types in ways comparable to the segregated activities of the C.I.A.M. of which he was to be an American delegate, Rush City represents remarkably involved and responsive designing in that heroic period of modern architecture and planning that is today so often characterized as "reductionist."

There was another American visionary plan of those years by Arthur Comey (1886–1954), a Harvard University professor of planning who was usually concerned with detailed, almost legalistic growth-plans for specific communities. Irritated by the utopianism and rigidity about size of settlement exhibited by the world-wide Garden City movement, Comey suggested not just a regional, but actually a national plan; he based it on a triangular arterial transportation network with hexagonal city areas laid out on synapses at the intersection of the diagonals of the triangular network *(fig. 16)*. The hexagons are, of course, harmonious with the triangles of

which they are composed and vice versa. This schema carries none of Neutra's social and familial concerns, but it does prefigure the geometry of areal economists like Walther Christaller, August Lösch, and Walter Izard, who for decades worked on what they called central place studies or "regional science." The drawings for Comey's project have not survived.

The works of Neutra and Comey both exemplify linear planning, that is, planning along efficient lines of transportation and transmission—in fact sub-optimizing such factors. Another important linear planner, Ludwig Hilberseimer (1885–1967), who was to insert the missing communal elements into linearism in his projects of the 1940s, in the 1920s—in addition to being an elegant and perhaps the most pristine characterizer of the modern movement[5]—produced one of the most overbearing projects we have ever seen with his *Hochhausstadt* (Skyscraper City). Hilberseimer later commented that this plan had been directed solely to solving problems of traffic planning. Certainly his later linear planning with branching community settlements (influenced by Miliutin, whom he knew) are more of the Neutra type, concentrating much attention on people's needs, low density occupancy, etc. Hilberseimer's original drawings for this particular project (for which we searched everywhere) have apparently disappeared.

It is, I think, by now clear that there are two opposite ways of presenting a visionary scheme: one, highly theoretical-professional and in style often schematic; the other, more popular, theatrical in character, often approaching what I call "magazine graphics" and even science fiction art. The versatile renderings of Hugh Ferriss (1889–1962) *(fig. 8)* are of the more popular type. He somehow had the ability to make a routine New York City skyscraper of his day look as if it were part of the City of God. He reminds us of Piranesi, Sant'Elia, and the Expressionist cinema of his time, but the way in which he envelops his subject in an exciting chiaroscuro is especially his. Note that it is precisely this dramatic shading that he added to Herbert Stevens's drawing *(fig. 89)*.

At this time (the '20s and '30s) Le Corbusier (1887–1965) developed his successive schemes for city and regional

15. *Richard Neutra, Rush City Reformed, (1923).*
No. 79.
16. *Arthur Comey, Diagram of Cardinal Arterial System of a
Nation,* Landscape Architecture, *January 1923.*
17. *Le Corbusier lecturing to architecture students and drawing
our No. 66, at Columbia University, April 1961.*

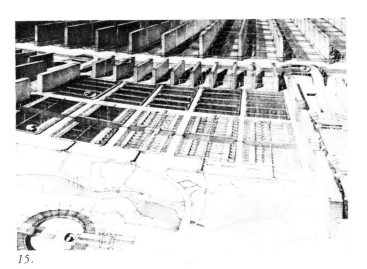

15.

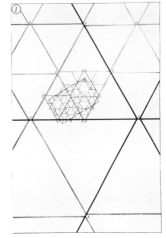

16.

17.

18. *Lloyd Wright, Civic Center Project for Los Angeles, 1925, as prepared for newspaper article.* No. 129.
19. *Lloyd Wright, Sketches for 1,000-foot-high City of the Future, 1926.* No. 130.
20. *Eric Mendelsohn, Untitled Drawing, January 1953.* No. 75.
21. *Mendelsohn lecturing and making drawings, including our Nos. 75-77, at the University of Oregon, January 1953.*
22. *Louis Kahn, Penn Center Project, 1957,* No. 41.

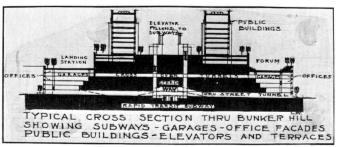

18.

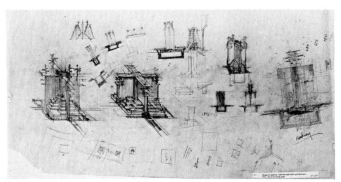

19.

22.

20.

planning: the City for 3 Million of the early 1920s, the Ville Radieuse of the early 1930s, the Radiant Farm and Linear Industrial City of the early 1940s. All of these figure in one way or another on the large butcher-paper sheets that he drew on his two visits to Columbia University in 1935 and 1961 (*fig. 17*). The earlier drawing, some twenty feet long, is almost a slide show of the lecture on the Ville Radieuse (Radiant City) that he gave several times on his 1935–36 trip to the U.S.A., recounted in his *When the Cathedrals Were White*. By the later date, albeit disillusioned somewhat in his utopianism, he still thought, spoke, and effortlessly sketched his vision of the linear city.

Interestingly enough, it was in the same worldwide depression years (later '20s, early '30s) that Frank Lloyd Wright (1867–1959) conceived, drew, and built a model for his image of the democratic American countryside, Broadacre City. It was envisaged on a national scale and schematically like Comey's network, but an enormous infill of social, philosophical, and functioning detail lay behind it, churned out by Wright in lectures and publications over the years. It was predictive of the *unregulated* spread of America's broad acres after World War II, but actually stands apart as one of the uniquely original planning visions of all time. We were unable to borrow drawings of it, in part because of Wright's own lifelong sense of his own uniqueness; we quote from Mr. Bruce Brooks Pfeiffer, Director of Archives at the Frank Lloyd Wright Memorial Foundation at Taliesin: "It was a long-standing principle throughout Mr. Wright's lifetime not to let his work be grouped together in exhibitions with Mies van der Rohe, Le Corbusier, etc. I am sure you can see how we are bound to continue to honor his feelings on this particular aspect of the exhibition of his work." Instead we show drawings from the domestic side of Broadacre City (*fig. 1*), what Wright called "Usonia." The term applied both to Wright's utopian notion of community conduct and to the house form itself, very economic and "a delightful association with sun, sky, surrounding gardens, and neighbors." The Auerbach house was designed on the triangular module for a member family of a Rochdale community in Westchester County, N.Y., that had been brought together in the early 1940s by a young devotee of Wright, David T. Henken, in order to establish a Usonian settlement based on the Broadacre theory. The Auerbach house was never built because it proved to be too expensive for the family even after

Wright had reduced the modular dimensions. Even if the house had been built along with the many others now in Pleasantville Usonia, the drawings for it would still represent a vision, as we have already pointed out.

It is instructive to compare the projects of Lloyd Wright (1890–1978), eldest son of Frank Lloyd Wright, with others who were then active in Southern California, notably his father, whose anti-skyscraper decentralist ideas began to germinate there in the mid '20s, and Neutra's team, which was at the same time starting on their decade of Rush City studies. Lloyd Wright applied his visions to the Los Angeles area much as others did to New York City, Paris, or Milan—metropolises with a concern for civic art but with severe circulation problems. In August 1925 the *Los Angeles Times* published Lloyd Wright's Civic Center Scheme (*fig. 18*), a multi-level arrangement that reminds one of Sant'Elia and Le Corbusier but is clearly a Wrightian cross-axial layout with almost Art Deco trimming in its elevation. The following year the *Times* published his plan for a spectacular 1000-foot-high, 40-story skyscraper city—anticipating his father's Mile-High "Illinois" building—with dirigible masts on top and landing fields below. The newspaper drawing for this has been lost, but we have on exhibition a series of sketches for it (*fig. 19*).

Following World War II the visionary revived, ostensibly stimulated by reconstruction programs and the desire to invent structures that would keep people safe from atomic attack, leading in the latter instance to radical decentralization plans and even underground living schemes. Then a tremendous surge occurred during the 1960s, a period of great building activity and belief that anything was possible.

Our drawings by Eric Mendelsohn (1887–1953) are post-World War II but actually continue his characteristic Expressionist shorthand method with its dramatic oblique perspective and often an over-arching curve that focuses like a lens on the contents. As he himself scribbled on one (*fig. 20*), "I write as I speak; I sketch as I write." As we do not have any record of what he said on this occasion—a visit to the University of Oregon in January 1953 (*fig. 21*)—and all his sketches always look "visionary," one is never sure which of his drawings represent a future building, a past structure or

24.

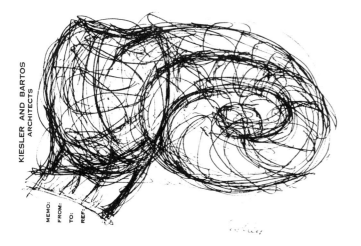

KIESLER AND BARTOS
ARCHITECTS

MEMO:
FROM:
TO:
REF:

23.

project, or a totally utopian concept. Those which he is drawing in the photograph seem to be related to past buildings of his, so we have selected three others that seem to be primarily visionary or look like his World University project of 1943, about which he said (at U.C.L.A. in March 1948), "I live in my visions and for my art. There seems to be no end to it."

The visions of Louis I. Kahn (1902–74) are, on the other hand, more specific in intent and recognizably so. We exhibit small sketches for his Penn Center in Philadelphia (*fig. 22*), part of studies which he made over a number of years, these being of his second-phase projects (1956–57). In *fig. 22* he has inserted his space-frame city tower in the form that he had worked out with Anne Griswold Tyng and which is on view as well (*fig. 72*). There was also probably input here from his close friend and colleague, Robert Le Ricolais, whose work is also in our exhibition.

The 1950s represent a period of individualism, whereas the 1960s tend to become a period of groups or schools that sought to devise new "modern movements" to replace those of the 1920s/30s. Architects and planners of the 1950s tended to think of themselves as furthering or amplifying their inherited traditions.

So it was with the architect Frederick Kiesler (1890–1965). Austrian born, Kiesler was an innovative designer who operated as a total artist, considering himself also to be a sculptor and a furniture designer; his projects do indeed incorporate both of these tendencies with the architectural. We exhibit two of his projects, a house and a theater, in both of which he had a lifelong interest. In fact, earlier studies than those we show for the "Endless" (*fig. 23*) were actually for a theater building. Kiesler's thought-sketches are so shorthand in character that we have found it necessary to include a photograph of his 1961 model of this project (*fig. 24*) to allow the viewer to determine whether the drawings are indeed stages in arriving at architecture. Kiesler remarked in the 1960s: "My definition of architecture is very simple: architecture is the art of making the superfluous necessary and building and shelter is the art of making the necessary superfluous."[6] We have included his theater in part because of the attention that the visionaries so often centered on theaters.

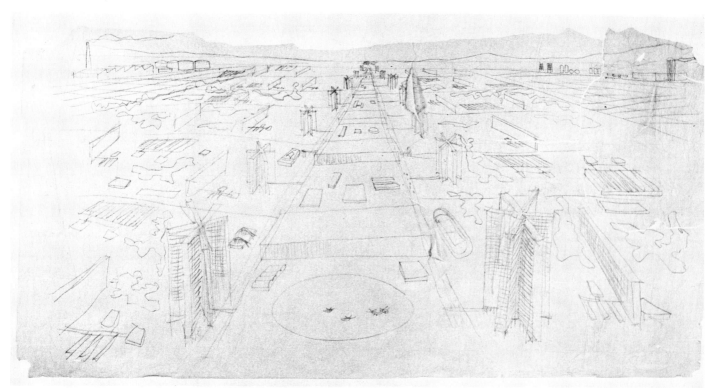

26.

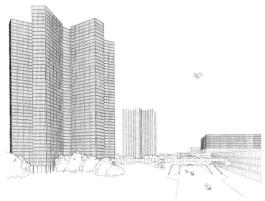

25.

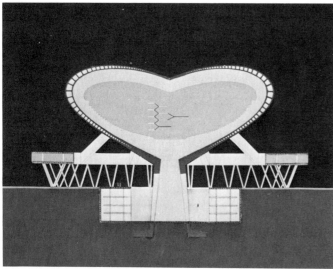

27.

31.

Others practice a tighter style of rendering, notably Reginald Malcolmson (1912–), an Irish-American colleague of Mies who admired and acquired Malcolmson drawings as well as clearly influencing him. Malcolmson is a "professional visionary" and has exhibited as such. His drawings are minimally rendered but are deeply expressive of both structure and meaning (i.e., function), while being at the same time formalistic. Among those we have selected from his repertoire are an early, rather Miesian, perspective of his Metrolinear City *(fig. 25)* and a later sketched study for the construction of a model of the project *(fig. 26)*.

The theater as performance hall again figures in the drawings of Amancio Williams (1913–), Argentine architect and colleague of Malcolmson. In this case the diagrammatic renderings were selected because of the designer's vision of acoustical efficiency *(figs. 27, 96)*. Again we note a preciseness of effect. The project is of a structure ideal in form since it is arrived at by the revolution of a curve around the central vertical axis, and perfect both in acoustics and visibility for the thousands of spectators that it would hold.

And then there are those whom we might call *technicians,* who are professionally either engineers or verging on that designation, although they are so cross-disciplinary in their activities and so curious about what precisely are the relationships between man, nature, science, and building that perhaps they would best be called *metaphysicians.*

Buckminster Fuller (1895–) is of this spirit. Fuller moves and thinks so fast that apparently he has not been careful about saving his drawings, but we were able to obtain some very contrasting types. From 1927 is the "mimeo sketch" which presents in comic-strip sequence a dirigible bombing a hole and implanting a ten-deck building in it *(fig. 28)*. This "drawing" is the only print left of a design that Fuller sketched on a mimeograph stencil. Our other examples of his projects are quite different in technique, both done in collaboration with his partner Shoji Sadao, who did the renderings. For instance, that for Triton City, a floating new town to accommodate about 100,000 people at the seacoast near crowded cities on the littoral, is an attractive example of modern office rendering skill relying on zipatone for its effect—that is to say, a collage *(fig. 29)*. We also illustrate it in model form *(fig. 30)*.

30.

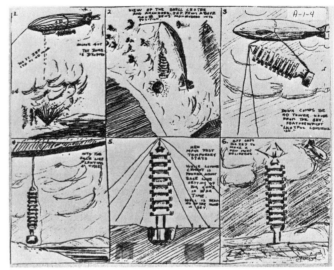

28.

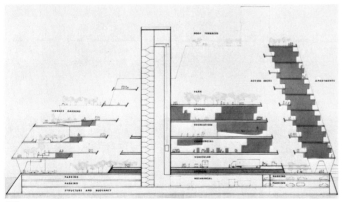

29.

32. *Konrad Wachsmann, Multi-level structure assembled from structural elements of a single type, 1953. No. 110.*
33. *Soleri, Cantilever Bridge, 1962. No. 97.*
34. *Anne Griswold Tyng, Urban Hierarchy diagram illustrating: a) Bilateral and rotational symmetries, b) Randomized helical symmetry, c) Spiral symmetry, d) Large-scale bilateral symmetry, 1970. Nos. 103-106.*

32.

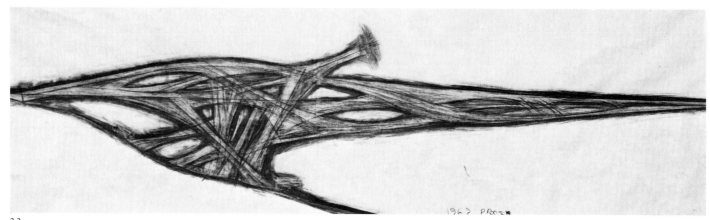

33.

Another highly technical vision is that of the engineer Herbert H. Stevens Jr., (1913–), early designer of air-supported structures, in this case for an airplane factory (1942) with a thin steel membrane roof supported by a pressure differential between inside and out *(fig. 31)*. Stevens held the first American patent for pneumatic structures of this kind, and went on a few years later to design a covered stadium with a seating capacity of 100,000 in Baltimore for a group headed by Glenn L. Martin, the airplane designer. As a theoretician, Stevens has also written on a number of metaphysical issues not related to engineering.

Quite philosophical as well is Konrad Wachsmann (1901–) whose book, *The Turning Point in Building: Structure and Design* has been for two decades a classic in architectural libraries. His interest in materials, geometry, standardization, joints, and performance has led him into fascinating projects of which we exhibit two examples; one is a study of linkage systems that in the drawing make up a multi-story structure *(fig. 32)*. Both of his projects date from the 1950s.

A grand master of such geometry/nature/structure relationships was the engineer Robert Le Ricolais (1894–1977). Trained in France, and a teacher at the University of Pennsylvania School of Architecture where he was close to Louis Kahn, Le Ricolais was interested in basic geometric units, especially as related to light space-frames that are achieved by the adroit employment of tension and compression members. We have chosen a group of his drawings that illustrate his fascination with geometric modules and with both the crystalline and organic forms that are thought to underlie the appearance of Nature *(figs. 4, 78)*.

The outburst of visionary projects in the 1960s was accompanied by a plethora of publications bearing titles "of the future," "of fantasy," "town and revolution," "l'avenir des villes," "experimental . . . ," "kinetic . . . ," "les visionnaires . . ."; architectural periodicals put out many special issues or sections devoted to the visionary.

Paolo Soleri (1919–) is representative of what happened. He unleashed enormous and fabulous projects with metaphorical names—most of them megastructures looking for all the world like geological crystals or automobile gear boxes. These were to be made habitable for men through a process he referred to as "miniaturization." But meanwhile he set to

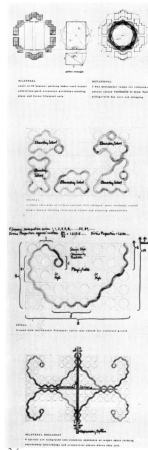

34.

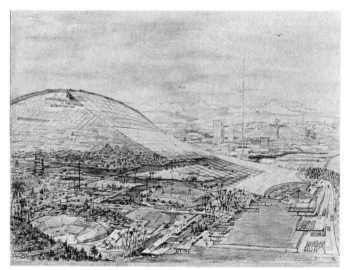

35.

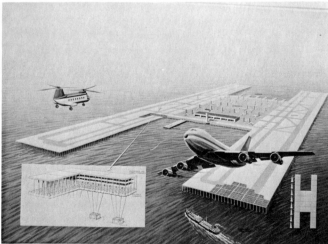

36.

work in the Arizona desert to build one of his projects, called "Arcosanti," by hand, with a commune of young workers, the sound of his beautifully crafted bells in their ears. His renderings are pristine, his preparatory sketches remarkably free and sometimes stretching endlessly on butcher-paper (*fig. 88*). They range from brief, concise, almost understatements (*fig. 33*) to long series that vary from schematic diagrams to specific forms. As he has said about his own sketch books: "Another explanation is that there is no such thing as the complete, final, or perfect response to any challenge, even when the challenge is specific and detailed. As soon as the first idea works itself onto paper, all its scarcely known relatives with different degrees of legitimacy are in close pursuit. So there they come sketchy and naked, to be picked up again later for reassessment and characterization."

Another outstanding individualist in a decade that I have described as consisting largely of groups or schools is Anne Griswold Tyng (1920–). Anne Tyng, mentioned earlier as an associate of Louis Kahn, works with modules, modulars, and the Platonic solids in a cosmological way that recalls both the ancients and the medieval master masons (*fig. 34*). Her reasoning is complex and synthesizing as she seeks out the compositional/geometric bases (bilateral, rotational, helical, and spiral) that determine natural and built form and that also reveal the formal cycles through which the history of building has passed.

Engineers in the 1960s have also indulged in fantasy, although they firmly deny it, insisting that everything they suggest and calculate is eminently possible.[7] This may be true, but the possible is not necessarily probable—another aspect of "what is the visionary"! Furthermore, these engineers insist that their *drawings* are only *part* of the development of any project, as they depend so heavily on constructed models both to illustrate their ideas and to run tests on them. However, dream they do, and we have on exhibition such visions by Frei Otto (1925–) of Germany and the Weidlinger Associates of the United States. Otto, famous for his tented structures, has on occasion suggested their use to construct huge artificial environments in areas of the globe where living and working are to take place under difficult environmental conditions (*fig. 35*). Weidlinger Associates' floating airport "FLAIR" (unbuilt) also takes on a visionary

37. *Superstudio, The Continuous Monument: "St. Moritz revisited," 1969. No. 102.*

37.

and fantastic flavor, especially in the way it was presented in the magazine *Popular Science (fig. 36)*.

The major groups of avant garde visionaries of the 1960s flourished in the United Kingdom (Archigram), Italy (Superstudio), Austria (albeit some of them working elsewhere), France, and Japan (the Metabolists). These *dramates personae* put on such a delightful charade in those years that I prefer not to describe the individuals in detail, but rather to let their drawings speak for themselves.

Archigram was perhaps the loudest with its Pop imagery and comic-strip renderings camouflaging an underlying serious, revolutionary intent to achieve a dynamic culture not unlike that of Sant'Elia—a throwaway civilization of consumption in which the obsolescent is discarded or torn down to be replaced by the new, itself of short life span *(figs. 52, 62, 69, 93)*.

Superstudio of Florence was in a sense the opposite. When not conceptualists, i.e., dealing with architecture that is only a written statement about itself, they were generally formalists, producing designs of endless geometric regularity, or designing collages like the Continuous Monument *(figs. 37, 90)*, which show pristine geometric forms stepping or stretching over the entire world, city and country.

The Austrians have some of the same fixation on pure geometric form: whether it be Friedrich St. Florian (1932–) with his tower city extending endlessly up into space *(fig. 38)*, Raimund Abraham (1933–) whose glacier city infills a mountain valley *(fig. 39)*, or Hans Hollein (1934–), tongue-in-cheek, suggesting that a sparkplug (!) is a skyscraper on the horizon *(fig. 40)*. We have none of the drawings of Walter Pichler (1936–) on exhibit, unfortunately.

The French seem like a group by virtue of the way in which they were published as ensemble by Michel Ragon and André Bloc. Of the considerable number of them we have on exhibition Claude Parent and Yona Friedman, both born in 1923. Friedman's Spatial City is a space-frame megastructure hovering high in the air in order to save the earth's surface for vegetation and to preserve historic buildings *(fig. 41)*. It seems mechanical and authoritarian, but the fact is that

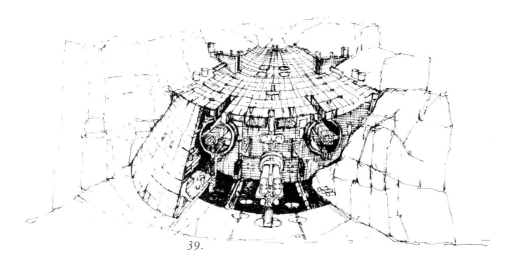

40.

39.

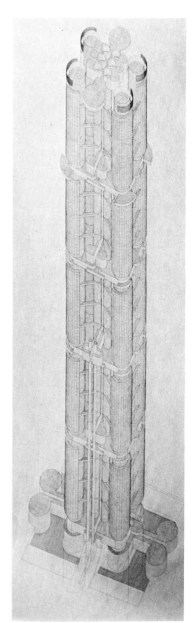

38.

42.

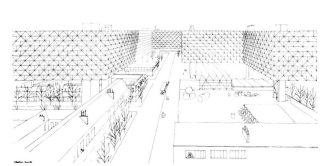

41.

43. *Noriaki Kurokawa, Porous Space Study, 1963/64.*
No. 58.
44. *Arata Isozaki, "Trees become Forest," 1960-62. No. 32.*
45. *Isozaki, Clusters in the Air, 1960-62. No. 34.*
46. *Kurokawa, Helix Structure, 1960-61. No. 55.*

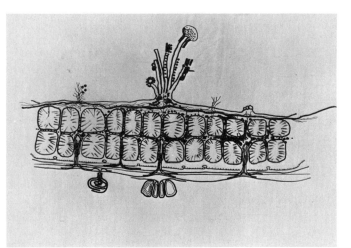

43.

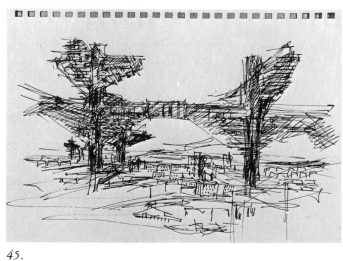

45.

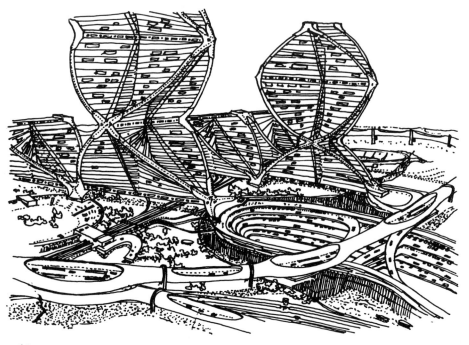

46.

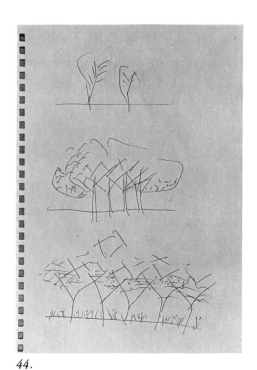

44.

Friedman takes the most meticulous care in working out precisely how the dwellings should be placed on the support structure to achieve optimal community interrelationships and how they should be arranged internally to fit the habitual routines of their residents. Parent's designs are for oblique—that is diagonally-arranged—megastructures, terraced as was popular among the French visionaries, although never more dramatically rendered and described than by him *(fig. 42)*.

Of the visionaries of the 1960s, the Japanese Metabolists presented what was perhaps the most explicit and serious program. They were convinced that life, design, and building share a dynamic process of change, from which the group took its name. There is an explicit organicism to be found in the Japanese drawings, for example, those of Kisho Kurokawa (1934–) *(fig. 43)* and Arata Isozaki (1931–) *(fig. 44)*. This concept of change also involved a certain traditionalism, a faithfulness to Japanese history and religion, that resulted in efforts to echo symbolic shapes like roofs in their designs *(fig. 45)*; to follow the tradition of the Shinto shrine involves periodic demolition and rebuilding which in turn echoes the obsolescence principle of the British Archigram group by which the Japanese were considerably influenced. Even certain radical projects of the Metabolists such as their towering interconnected megastructures to free the ground for agriculture *(fig. 46)* and their offshore floating cities *(fig. 47)* are in general in a Japanese tradition of the preciousness of land and the desire to gain more at any cost. The endless care that Kiyonori Kikutake (1928–) took with the designing of his tower and floating cities and then their eventual joining together *(fig. 48)* reveals that the Metabolists were far more pragmatic than is suggested by some of their early metaphorical polemics, so characteristic of the 1960s movements. What we seem to have in the Metabolists' argumentation and drawings of the 1960s—however bizarre—was an architectual/urban theoretical framework that has already turned some futurist visions of capsule towers and floating platforms into actuality and indicates what we may increasingly see in built structures by them.

IV

As this exhibition includes a wide range of architectural drawings, I think that the matter of categories, use,

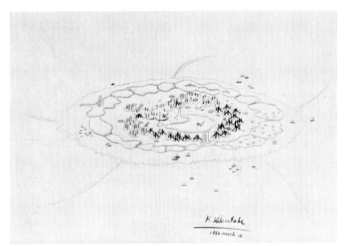

47.

48.

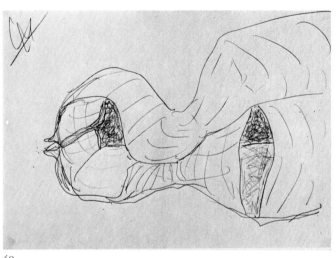

49.

meaning, and artistry of such drawings deserves some discussion.

Again we run into the difficulties of defining what "visionary" means. On a day-to-day basis any drawing for a particular structure, except perhaps a working drawing, could be called a "vision" or prophecy of what the eventual result will be. Or, on the other hand, a section or a groundplan of an edifice is a vision, or mode of vision, of the edifice that exists only as a concept, however real; and it takes some instruction for the layman to realize that an orthographic plan or section (see below) is not just a magical diagram or a figment of the designer's imagination.

Furthermore, as we have already noted, the drawings on exhibition range from very precise "presentation" drawings of improbable situations made on the drawing board *(fig. 12)* to quick scribbles on a sketching pad that we must almost take on faith to represent any building at all *(figs. 23, 49)*. Knowing that Kiesler considered himself to be a sculptor as well, perhaps his sketches are works of art in their own right and not merely preliminaries for a future piece of architecture. So we have works on paper that can be "paper art," and we have works on paper which might be called "paper architecture" *(fig. 2)* or a "paper city." Or again, even among the professional delineators of architecture like Hugh Ferriss *(fig. 50)* we can see that the drawing is a repository of ideas or even poetry more significant for the future than the particular building that may have inspired Ferriss to the vision. Buildings like that *were* going up when Ferriss was drawing them; perhaps this is a visionary drawing "after the fact," a Shangri-La that already existed and needed only to be revealed.

What we are dealing with, then, is a paper architecture of one sort or another, and just as architecture and cities have their purpose or function, their mode of assemblage, and their design, i.e., artistic principles, so do architectural drawings. An architectural drawing may be analyzed or classified according to its own design or geometry, its function (that is, its place in the architectural designing process), or its materials and technique, i.e., its assemblage.

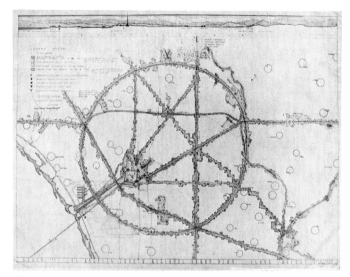

51.

50.

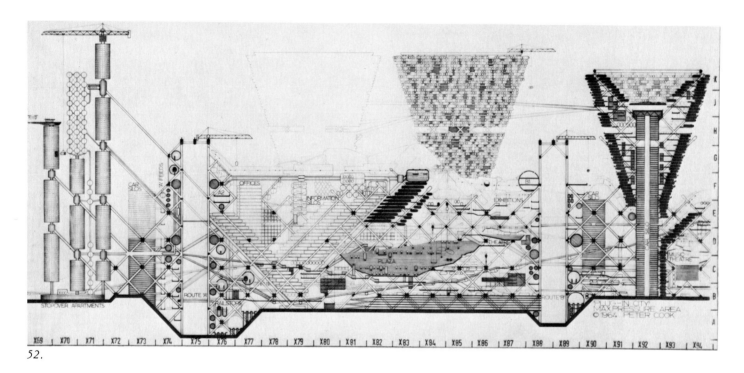

52.

54.

Design or appearance can be communicated in a drawing by orthographic projection, meaning seen "straight on" with the dimensions of parts in the drawing "true"; by perspective, or *scenografia* as the Renaissance called it, with the parts diminishing in size toward the vanishing point or points; or by a cutaway that shows exterior and interior parts simultaneously and may or may not be in perspective. These are essentially characterizations of the geometrical nature of drawings.

The basic types of orthographic drawings—and they often carry a scale—are: 1) the elevation *(fig. 81)* which usually reveals layers or depth, in this case by means of shading. 2) Plans, e.g., horizontal sections—which, if a ground plan, used to be called *ichnografia* from the Greek word for footprint. 3) A site or regional plan, which is essentially an extension of this *(fig. 51)*. 4) The section *(fig. 52)* which, like an elevation, often adds things that can be seen behind the sectional cut *(fig. 54)*.

Perspective elevations may be of single-point convergence, which tends to be descriptive *(fig. 25)*, or multiple-point and hence oblique and dramatic *(fig. 5)*—a specialty of Mendelsohn *(fig. 53)*. There are different degrees of overshot perspectives, depending on the purpose: simple overshot as in *(fig. 39)*, a bird's-eye view looking down from a considerable height *(fig. 2)*, and its opposite, a worm's-eye view looking up from underneath through the ground plan (usually indicated), a device that Auguste Choisy used to great advantage. We do not have an example on exhibition (but see *fig. 32*).

Then there are cutaways, which the last type also represents. These may be done in a general perspective that suggests both vertical sections and floor plans of the structure *(fig. 61)*. Common, especially in recent years, are isometric cutaways in which dimensions of depicted objects are in true scale and the receding sides of objects do not converge. A special type of isometric, the axonometric rendering *(figs. 38, 62)* also has the angles of all horizontal sections true (i.e., usually 90°), and thus is essentially a three-dimensional model in projection. There are numerous examples of this in the exhibition.

As regards classification of drawings according to their use in the process of designing things, one starts with *sketches* which may be (1) simply of ideas, i.e., referential *(figs. 6, 23)* or (2)

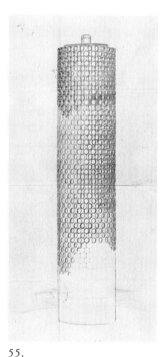

55.

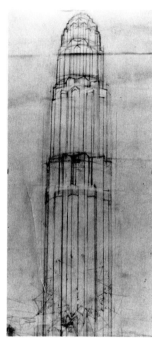

56.

53.

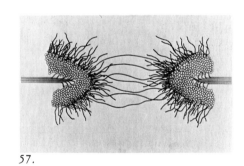

57.

59.

58.

57. *Kurokawa, Fiber Form Study, 1964-65.* No. 57.
58. *Le Corbusier, Drawings for a lecture on Linear Decentralization, April 1961.* No. 64.
59. *Andrew Weininger, Bauhaus student sketches, 1921, 1922.* Nos. 115-118. *The two right-hand ones were influenced by the presence of Theo van Doesburg.*

actual preparatory steps as are those by Kikutake in which *fig. 74* is a preliminary pair of study overlays for a tower which is then made in a drawn elevation *(fig. 55)*, photographed and mounted as a collage on a drawn view *(fig. 48)*. There are then *presentation* drawings which may be pictures like paintings *(fig. 10)*, or draughting-board efforts *(fig. 29)*, or may be popularized versions (as described above, *fig. 36*), or even be done in high contrast for a newspaper *(fig. 18)*. In preparation for presentation drawings all sorts of tracing paper and photographic processes may be used in the sense of overlays, in order to transfer elements to the final surface. Hugh Ferriss used such procedures very intricately, although his *(fig. 56)* seems rather to be a tracing-paper sketch and not an overlay. Konrad Wachsmann involves himself in endless and detailed technical procedures of this sort. He has even on occasion reduced photographically large drawings of joints to a tiny size and attached them to the verso of large thin-tracing-paper renderings of the total structure so that the joint details are accurate and can be seen through the tracing paper as part of the presentation rendering. Another process-type drawing is the diagram. Many drawings in our exhibition are diagrammatic or simplified; as we have pointed out, the visionary lends itself to this. But diagrams have their use as an aid to the designer in conceptualizing *(fig. 57)*, or as an effort to explain complexities in a simple manner *(fig. 34)*, or rhetorically as Le Corbusier did in his lecture-drawings *(fig. 58)*. Geometric explanations like Tyng's and geometric hypotheses like Le Ricolais's are obviously clearer when diagrammatic. In non-perspective periods of history visionary drawings have been invariably diagrammatic, for instance in the early Middle Ages; in fact, it might be said that diagrammatic drawings are a historic phase of depiction that preceded the invention of perspective.

There are certain other types of architectural drawings to mention. One is the school project, none of which is on exhibition here, but which did figure significantly in our recent publication, *Unbuilt America*. School projects are frequently visionary especially in the days of Beaux Arts curriculum; this visionary, impractical character has often led to student or faculty revolts in schools, demanding more practical projects related to actual working conditions. Tony Garnier's original *cité industrielle* project when submitted to the authorities of the Ecole des Beaux Arts aroused controversy because of its "practicality." But with the new workshop/

faculty/student pedagogy of advanced schools of the 1920s, a student's work would often reveal what was actually transpiring in the European avant garde. This is exemplified by the four student sketches of Andrew Weininger *(fig. 59)* that show the successive influence of Johannes Itten, his design teacher, and then Theo van Doesburg's intrusive de Stijl tendencies which were, of course, to take over in the Bauhaus. We do not include working drawings—which are made in detail, usually for the contractor and builder—although some in our exhibition, e.g., Webb's *(fig. 93)* might be taken as working drawings for a visionary project.

And there is the class of drawing produced by professional renderers or delineators. While it may be that a number of our presentation drawings were not made by the hand of the person to whom we have attributed them but rather by some draughtsman in an office, we do have several on view that are indeed professionally rendered. Hugh Ferriss often did drawings for others than himself, as for example for Stevens; one rendering of Charles Lamb's Streets in the Air was done by himself *(fig. 10)* but another was produced by his friend Vernon Howe Bailey. Bailey's rendering *(fig. 76)*, published in the *New York Herald* in 1908, was almost immediately adapted by a writer in the British periodical *The Architect and Contract Reporter* in a manner that caused Bailey to respond angrily in that magazine, accusing the writer of misrepresenting both himself and Lamb, and in a sense plagiarizing them. [8] So a delineator can come to identify himself quite thoroughly with the vision of the person for whom he is drawing.

Last to discuss about architectural drawings is the matter of how they were *done* as regards their techniques and materials. The range of materials should be clear from our catalogue entries: pencils, crayons, inks, pigments, and pastings (collage); on paper, board, cloth, skin, plastic. There are also reproductive processes such as the blueprint, ozalid, ditto machine, mimeograph, as well as drawings on photographs and photostats *(fig. 60)*, pasted photos and montages, and the new computer graphics.

And, finally, there is the matter of models, which have often displaced drawings in our century, especially when the qualities sought were basic elementary forms and spaces or in-scale devices that, as we observed, can be submitted to physical tests in various ways—for instance Gaudí's hanging

funicular cords or the use of plastic models photographed
under stress with polarized light. Among the exhibited
visionaries Fuller, Malcolmson, and Otto emphasize the
importance to them of models; Kenzo Tange employs models
from the first stages of his designs and seemingly de-values
drawings.[9] In fact, Malcolmson's *(fig. 26)* was not a sketch *of*
his project but rather a sketch in preparation for a *model* of it
that was then exhibited; Fuller/Sadao, like Michelangelo before
them, have no finished elevation of their Triton City, only a
model of which they have supplied us with a photograph for
the exhibition *(fig. 30)*. The use of models was particularly
marked in the Modern Movement; but these models did not
necessarily replace drawings, being rather complementary to
them, as described above.

In categorizing the types of architectural renderings in this
exhibition my purpose is not to be didactic, but to try to
explain in part the almost unintelligible diversity of drawings
that are employed for visionary purposes. It should be
understood that the wide range of drawing types and hands of
execution shown here were not chosen with a competitive
intent or qualitative comparison in mind. Much paper
architecture is for the solitary reasoning, philosophy, or
contemplation of the individuals who draw it, that is to say, a
private thing, and we may be doing some of the designers
injustice by exhibiting their drawings publicly rather than
judging the built structures—our interest is, then, to exhibit
the scope and variety of the visions, not to make judgments on
those whose insights they were.

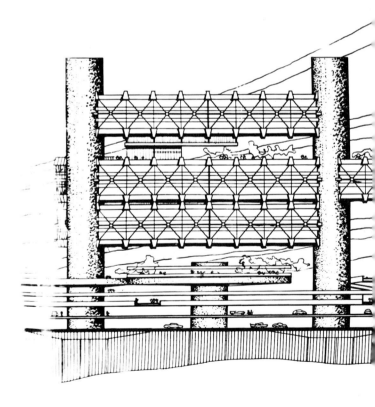

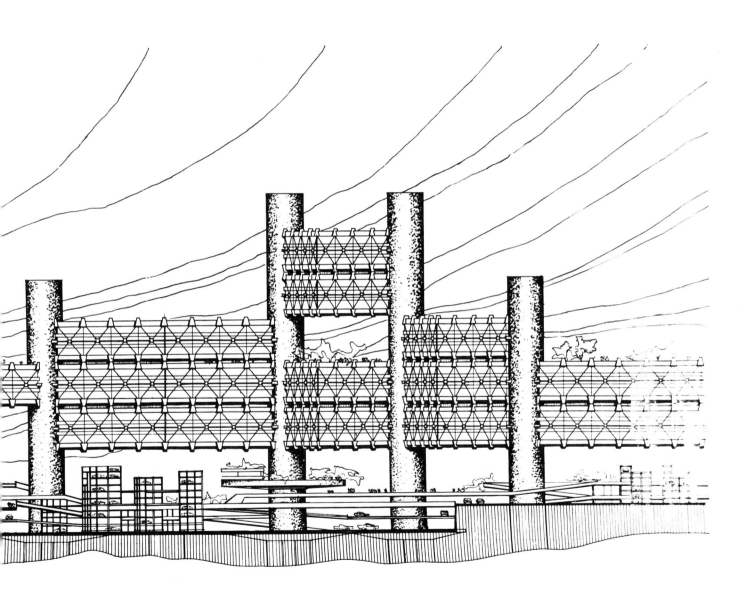

Abraham, Raimund (Lienz, Austria, 1933–)

Trained at the School of Architecture and Engineering of the Technical University of Graz, Austria, Abraham worked in Brussels and Vienna before coming to the United States in the late 1960s. He lived and worked in the studio of Frederick Kiesler in New York City in 1964 and taught at the Rhode Island School of Design from 1964 to 1971; he has served as visiting professor at the Architectural Association in London. Since 1971 he has worked as architect and designer in New York City, where he is a professor at the Cooper Union and the Pratt Institute.
Abraham began to develop Utopian architecture in Vienna in the early sixties at the same time as Walter Pichler, and has exhibited his drawings of it at the National Institute of Architects in Rome, the Museum of Modern Art in New York City (1967), the Milan Triennale (1968), the Architectural League of New York, the Moderna Museet of Stockholm (1969), and at the Venice Biennale (1976).
He has constructed experimental houses and schools in the United States and has received numerous awards for his work.

1 "Glacier City," linear environment, perspective cutaway *(fig. 39)*

Rendering, 1964
Ink and pencil on drawing paper, 8¼ x 15⅜" (21 x 39 cm.)
Unsigned
Lent by the Museum of Modern Art, New York City, Philip Johnson Fund

A concave, geometrically- and mechanically-articulated membrane, hung between the amorphous edges of a spacious, mountainous valley, provides shelter and a solar energy reflector for a continuously growing city along a complex network of services and transportation, without imposing a definite social structure.
Cavities of shadow and light create spatial cores between the amorphous topography of the valley and the technical and geometrized elements of the city. The growth of the city is limited only by the geographic boundaries of the valleys, in a manner similar to the expansion of historic glaciers.

2 "Universal City," bird's-eye perspective view

Rendering, 1966
Pen, ink, photomontage, and pencil on board, 17⅝ x 22⅛" (44.3 x 56.2 cm.)
Unsigned
Lent by the Museum of Modern Art, New York City, Philip Johnson Fund

The city is a continuous path and in its final form would encircle the globe, containing the entire urban population, while the continents would regenerate the original flora and fauna. Horizontal skyscrapers would form the spatial structure of the artificial valley of the city, interrupted at strategic points by diagonally-organized junctions, terminal points, and distribution centers. Conventional transportation is accessible to all dwellings while all mechanized and automatized transportation systems would run at the bottom surface of the valley.

3 "Megabridge," perspective cutaway *(fig. 61)*

The bridge as a total linear building with central arteries of conventional and automatized transportation systems encapsulated by concentric layers of dwelling units that form horizontal cylinders articulated by vertical junctions serving as interchanges between water and bridge or land and bridge.

4 "Transplantation 1," underwater city, cutaway view

Rendering, 1967
Photomontage with colored pencil on board, 13½ x 17¼" (34.3 x 43.8 cm.)
Initialed "R. A. '67"
Lent by the Museum of Modern Art, New York City, Philip Johnson Fund

The site of an existing salt plant forms a winding path around a center and gradually recedes from it, revealing a central nucleus which becomes the gate to a vertical city reaching towards the bottom of the ocean. A machine-like organism of concentric metallic skins forms a protective shelter for the soft core of the inner parts of the city, emitting light to make it glow in the darkness of the sea.

The Vision of the City, 1962
(Translated from the German by the author)

Cities
altars of mechanical intestines
split open abysses
radiating tunnels
piled up
earthen containers
humans on rollers
spheres
kinetic volumes
in space
moving sidewards
without direction
encapsulated
by the darkness
of ever growing plants
crystallized
pulsating in
continuous movement
of the subterranean parts
of mechanized spectacles
displaying the corpses of
animals
plants
humans
laying out in space
elevated above
the wonderful chaos
of concrete cubes
cones
sewers
cathedrals
brothels beneath the surface
slaughterhouses
coffins on conveyors
windowless
at the bottom of sun craters
buildings on the crossroads
circular buildings
cantilevers
without function
junctions
of cylindric
linear bridges
penetrating
mountains of luminous spheres
radiating
artificial rainbows
vertical buildings
growing
toward the light
of mechanical suns
senseless
empty planes
streets
rings of gallows
encircling
the gigantic womb
of the inner parts
of the city

Raimund Abraham

61. *Abraham, Megabridge, No. 3.*

Rendering, 1965
Ink on paper on acrylic background
Signed: "Abraham '65"
Lent by Raimund Abraham

Cook, Peter (Southend-on-Sea, England, 1936-)

Most visible member of the Archigram group, Peter Cook edits the group's publications and originated its graphic style. He is Archigram's moving spirit: talkative, energetic, and a talented PR man.

He grew up in Bournemouth, where he began his architectural studies, before going to study at the Architectural Association. In London in the late '50s and early '60s he began to meet the people who eventually banded together as Archigram, and who published Archigram I in May of 1961.

Peter Cook has been on the faculty of the Architectural Association as fifth-year master since 1965. He lectures and teaches, and recently was asked by Japan Architect to judge its housing competition. He draws constantly, and is an avid fan of classical music (in particular of Mahler). He is reputed to be capable of whistling symphonies on request.

5 Plug-in City, axonometric view *(fig. 62)*

6 Plug-in City, section of Maximum Pressure Area *(fig. 52)*

Rendering, 1964
Ink on paper, 20¼ x 44½" (51.4 x 113 cm.)
Labeled: "© 1964 Peter Cook"
Lent by Gilman Paper Co.

At a casual glance the Plug-in City appears to be a common or garden variety megastructure: here are the familiar diagonals of the load-bearing frame, there the prefabricated infill cells. In fact, nothing could be farther from the intent than to present a blueprint for another orderly and tedious mega-city.

The Plug-in City is as open-ended a structure as Peter Cook's considerable ingenuity can invent. It has no definitive form. Instead it has an anarchic plan reminiscent of the layout of a medieval town, which is hardly surprising, as the purpose is to produce a city with as dynamic and unregulated a response to human social needs as the medieval city (is supposed to have) possessed. As little as possible is pre-determined, in order to allow the "greatest possible scope for growth and regeneration." In fact the entire city is intended to replace itself, with the aid of its omnipresent cranes, every 40 years. There is meant to be a constant activity of swapping new bits for old, as new technologies and needs make existing facilities obsolete.

A city which can extend, exchange, remove itself without affecting its ultimate stability is the paramount goal. But as usual with Archigram the secondary goal is to have a good time; they themselves say they do it all "for a bit of a giggle." The exuberant variety of building forms in the City, the loving attention given to tiny units dangling at cranesend waiting to be popped into the nearest available hole, the hovering office buildings scampering about the river like so many robotic mice—all are calculated attempts to escape from architectural dreariness.

The futuristic trappings are all part of the fun, but they are equally part of the message. Architecture is not permanent; the passwords are expendability, indeterminacy, exchange, and removal. What Archigram really wants is an architecture that responds to human desires as they occur. Plug-in City is an intermediate step toward that true adaptability in which hidden networks will respond to thought waves and environment will be limited only by individual imagination.

Janet White

62. Cook, *Plug-in City*, No. 5.

Rendering, 1964
Mixed media on cardboard, 27½ x 30" (69.8 x 76.2 cm.)
Signed on back.
Lent by Gilman Paper Co.

Ferriss, Hugh (St. Louis, 1889—New York City, 1962)

From the 1920s until his death in 1962, Hugh Ferriss was one of America's foremost architectural delineators. After his graduation in 1911 from the Beaux Arts-oriented school of architecture at Washington University (an important exhibition of his drawings was held at his alma mater in 1976), he moved to New York City where he worked as draughtsman for three years, without pay, in the office of Cass Gilbert. In 1915 he started private practice as an architectural renderer; his drawings catalogue many of the major structures erected in America over the course of his long and successful career. In the capacity of consultant, he also contributed to the design of important projects such as the 1939 World's Fair and the United Nations Headquarters, both in New York.
Ferriss's dramatic chiaroscuro interpretations of the skyscrapers of the 1920s have become visual synonyms for the term "Art Deco" architecture. Particularly influential were the zoning envelope studies, executed in collaboration with the architect Harvey Wiley Corbett, which emphasized the beauty and power inherent in the set-back form for tall buildings prescribed by the 1916 New York zoning law. Although he never built a building, Ferriss was the architect of a visionary city, visualized in his 1929 book The Metropolis of Tomorrow. *The drawings in this book express Ferriss's optimism about the ability of architecture and technology to create a better world.*

7 "Buildings like Mountains," elevation *(fig. 50)*

Rendering, 1925
Graphite on illustration board, varnished, 11 x 8½" (28.0 x 22.5 cm.)
Signed: "Hugh Ferriss"
Lent by Ferdinand Eiseman, New York City

8 "The Lure of the City," panoramic view *(fig. 8)*

Rendering, c. 1925
Charcoal on paper, 20¼ x 26¼" (51.4 x 66.7 cm.)
Signed: "To Ann, December 22, 1932/Hugh Ferriss" (given to the artist's niece as a wedding present)
Lent by Mrs. Ann Ferriss Harris, Mystic, Connecticut

In "The Lure of the City" (*The Metropolis of Tomorrow*, p. 58), Ferriss invites the viewer to wonder with him at the grandeur of the city and the magic of its towers, which in this drawing stretch beyond the upper limits of the paper. "Buildings like Mountains" (*Metropolis*, frontispiece) suggests the strength and solidity of the colossal new buildings.[10] This drawing is particularly interesting because its concept of a building as an undefined mass relates to the first stage in Ferriss's process of rendering, which he described in detail in a number of articles over his career. He wrote, "From the renderer's point of view a building is in the first place, a material mass . . . and while in the constructing of a building this effect may be the last to be realized, in the drawing of a building, logically it is the first . . . . The draughtsman's best procedure is first to delineate the essentials of his subject, then to build all indications of detail on this foundation."[11]
Ferriss's usual method was first to sketch in a few lines with a soft pencil or charcoal to indicate the mass, then to "confirm and solidify these outlines by introducing tone values—produced by drawing, rapidly, a number of freehand lines across the areas to be shaded and rubbing these lines together into a tone with a gloved finger or a paper stump."[12] A kneaded eraser could then be used to pick out the highlights.

9 "Philosophy," elevation and plan *(fig. 56)*

Sketch, c. 1928
Pencil on tracing paper, 40½ x 22" (102.2 x 56 cm.)
Unsigned
Lent by the Avery Architectural Library, Columbia University

Rendering, 1928
Charcoal on paper, 38 x 22" (96.5 x 55.9 cm.)
Signed: "Hugh Ferriss 1928"
Lent by the Avery Architectural Library, Columbia University

10 "Philosophy," elevation   *(fig. 63)*

The drawing and sketch for "Philosophy" (*Metropolis,* p. 136) show a tower to be located at the point where the Art and Science zones of Ferriss's visionary city plan meet. The faceted form of the glass tower, which recalls the German Expressionist designs of the Luckhardt brothers, Taut, and others, is generated in plan and elevation by a mystical numerology. Above the base, the shaft rises in seven stages in a ratio of 3:1:3. The plan of the building—a nine-pointed star, or three superimposed triangles—is indicated in pencil on the tracing paper study for the drawing *(fig. 56).* Ferriss intended the meaning of this building to remain enigmatic, for it was to be the Center of Philosophy in his city of the future.

In a long entry on architectural rendering which he authored in the 1936, 14th, edition of the *Encyclopaedia Britannica* (this article, dropped from the later editions, indicates the prestige of rendering in the 1930s), Ferriss wrote that the ideal rendering must convey the material, emotional, and intellectual facts of the subject. Even in commissioned illustrations, a delineator should aspire to be more than a mere copyist; he should interpret the architectural significance of the building. Beyond this, too, the renderer should assume even greater responsibilities in the future; "to serve as a guide in city planning, to assist in evolving new types of architecture, and to strengthen the psychological influence of architecture on human values."[13]

Ferriss also rendered and assisted with the drawings of Herbert H. Stevens, Jr., that are to be seen elsewhere in this exhibition.

Carol Willis

Finsterlin, Hermann (Munich, 1887—Stuttgart, 1974)

After studying physics, chemistry, and philosophy at the University of Munich, Finsterlin abandoned academic pursuits to become a painter. In 1919 he became a non-resident member of the Arbeitsrat für Kunst (Work Council on the Arts), an Expressionist group in Berlin. The exhibition "Unknown Architects," held under the auspices of the Arbeitsrat in 1919, included a room of Finsterlin drawings. In 1919-20 he was a member of Die Gläserne Kette (The Glass Chain), a utopian exchange of letters organized by Bruno Taut.

Finsterlin was one of the few painter members of the Arbeitsrat, created primarily by architects after the revolution of 1918 as a sounding board for new ideas in architecture. Because architectural commissions were difficult to come by during the immediate post-war period, the Arbeitsrat concentrated its efforts upon the creation of an ideal and highly experimental architecture. The projects that came out of the Arbeitsrat were to become quintessential Expressionist architecture.   Finsterlin's fluid drawing style, unhampered by exposure to architectural draughting techniques, was seen as a refreshing stimulus. His designs can be classified loosely as organic; Finsterlin himself wrote that they lie somewhere between the crystalline and the amorphous.[14] *Or, to quote Hans Luckhardt, a fellow member of the Arbeitsrat and Die Gläserne Kette, regarding Finsterlin's style: "Architecture should not imitate Nature, but must itself be Nature."*[15]

Although the two drawings "Concert Hall" and "Cathedral" bear a 1919 date and although certainly conceived in 1919, they were in all likelihood executed in 1964, the year in which Finsterlin gave them to me. This version of "Concert Hall" differs slightly from two other published versions.[16] *The same is true of "Cathedral."*[17] *Finsterlin, one of the few members of the Arbeitsrat still living during the '60s, became eager to supply historians with information about himself. This fact may account for the disproportionate representation of Finsterlin in the recent histories of Expressionism. (Borsi and König's* Architettura dell' Espressionismo *contains a whole chapter on Finsterlin.) Unfortunately, by this time his ability to recall details of his early career was often impaired. For instance, he claimed that it was he who had inspired Taut's vision of an alpine architecture;*[18] *however, Taut's* Alpine Architecture *had been conceived long before he met Finsterlin. Similarly, he wrote that he was called to lecture at the Bauhaus in 1932/33 by Hannes Meyer to counteract Miesian severity.*[19] *Since Mies himself was the director of the Bauhaus in these years, and because he left the Bauhaus in 1930, Finsterlin's contact with the Bauhaus must have occurred earlier.*[20]

11 Concert Hall, elevation   *(fig. 13)*

Sketch, 1919
Pencil, colored pencil, and watercolor on paper, 10 x 14⅛" (25.4 x 35.9 cm.)
Signed: "Finsterlin 1919"
Lent by: Professor Rosemarie Haag Bletter

A drawing almost identical with this one was illustrated in the correspondence of the Gläserne Kette in 1920 where Finsterlin described it thus: "Un-veined white marble covers the pyramid; the globular domes, movable in socket-joints, with polished smoky quartz windows and a casing of pale pink majolica"[21] There is no particular reason why this project was called a "Concert Hall"—it hardly seems to matter what building type we are dealing with in any of Finsterlin's designs, since their conception is non-specific. What his drawings do convey is a sensuousness of color and of materials and imaginative forms that exist totally outside the realm of functional necessity.

12 "Der Dom" (Cathedral), elevation   *(fig. 64)*

This "Cathedral" appears like some Ur-form deposited by a gigantic cataclysm, and not like a consciously articulated architecture. It is a spontaneous, intuitive design, the immediate practical application of which is irrelevant. Such projects were meant to stretch the imagination and were seen as an antidote to conventional design, associated with the pre-revolutionary period. A freeing from pragmatic constraint is also evidenced in the following words by Finsterlin: "Tell me, have you never been irritated by the brutal system of your six walls and by the intrusion of caskets for your thousand material necessities? Have you never… wished…to let your impulses play freely within the mellow substance of the stone?"[22]

Once architects returned from the high utopian expectations of the postwar period to real commissions, Finsterlin's designs lost their immediate power to inspire. For down-to-earth buildings they were too unbridled, amorphous, and out of touch with the social realities of the '20s. After his brief encounter with architecture Finsterlin moved on to the painting of oils and murals often of a lurid, erotic nature.

Rosemarie Haag Bletter

64. *Finsterlin, Cathedral, 1919. No. 12.*

Sketch, 1919
Pencil, colored pencil, and watercolor on paper, 10 x 14⅛" (25.4 x 35.9 cm.)
Signed: "Finsterlin 1919"
Lent by: Professor Rosemarie Haag Bletter

Friedman, Yona (Budapest, 1923–)

Trained in architecture at the Technological Institute in Haifa, Yona Friedman lives in Paris. Paris has been the inspiration and earthly base of many of his schemes for the Spatial City, the first of which he published there in 1958. He is discussed by Michel Ragon in his books and in the pages of L'Architecture d'aujourd'hui *as a member of the French megastructuralists who were exploring the possibilities of "urbanisme spatial" in the early 1960s. He has taught in the United States at Harvard, Princeton, the University of California, and the University of Michigan.*

For Friedman the lightweight space-frame is a version of his search for "an ideal infrastructure" that is applicable any place and any time. In an article in the Architects' Year Book *on "Urban Structures" in 1968 he explains:*

"We are facing a constantly changing world. These changes are difficult to foresee and their intensity as well as their direction is unpredictable. As town planning must include at least some foresight, it is especially affected by this situation. How should one plan, when one cannot know the way of life, nor the techniques which will be available only a few years ahead?

The only way that appears to be open for such a prevision would be to reduce planning criteria to a few, obviously unchanging facts: in other words, to fix the axioms of town living."

Such a neutral infrastructure that contains all the services that a city needs (power, water, communications, sewers) is then the framework for the realization of an age-old vision, that of mobility, changeability, and self-design for individual human beings in groupings of their choice.

Yona Friedman's super-scale cities intrigue with the leap to the microcosm of living units under individual control. This practical emphasis on self-design, which by 1974 he refers to and exhibits as "The Greatest Super Vision," makes Friedman special among the megastructuralists.

13 "Vue d'une ville spatiale" (View of a spatial city), bird's-eye

Freehand rendering, 1956
Ink on paper, 8 x 10" (20.3 x 25.4 cm.)
Unsigned
Lent by Gilman Paper Co.

The grid frame with its partially filled-in structures indicated with heavy black lines could extend endlessly over this featureless landscape. The irregular pattern of the heavy lines and the cut-out sections in the grid create a pleasing design that floats like a weightless carpet over a countryside barely indicated by intersecting roads. The thin supports do not touch the ground nor do they seem to carry a load, but dangle like sensors toward earth. This is truly a spatial city suspended in a space-time continuum.

14 Project for Paris, overview   *(fig. 41)*

Freehand rendering, 1959
Ink over pencil on paper, 18 x 25" (45.7 x 63.5 cm.)
Signed: "Y. Friedman 20.10.59"
Lent by Gilman Paper Co.

Space-frame supported by pilotis over a neighborhood of two-to-four-floor residential buildings in Paris. The pylons, spaced irregularly, are set into the open areas between the houses. Space-frame and supports are rendered schematically while the real Paris charms with homey touches including a cat trying to open a window. Above it all the sun, to indicate perhaps that Friedman's project will not prevent it from reaching the familiar streets.

The scheme of horizontal expansion on pylons containing vertical transportation and utilities is reminiscent of El Lissitsky's "Wolkenbügel" ("Sky-hooks") of the 1920s, although the resemblance is not so pronounced in this version by Friedman.

15 African City, elevation   *(fig. 65)*

A space-frame extending over a body of water supported by solid round and angular open pilotis. The floor has a series of rectangular openings or skylights. On the roof adjustable sails control the sunlight. A bright sun shines above the "City" which, however, casts no shadow on the bucolic, "primitive" landscape below. There is no attempt to integrate the high-tech spatial city with the idealized third-world ambient which includes native canoes, a smiling crocodile, a figure in Yoga pose, and a sailboat—all symbols of the unspoiled Africa of storybooks. Are we to take this seriously, or is Friedman teasing us as Paul Klee does in his drawing "African Village Scene," 1925?

Christiane C. Collins

Fuller, R. Buckminster (Milton, Mass., 1895–)

Architect, engineer, inventor, Fuller was essentially self-prepared in all these professions and for the over one hundred visiting professorships he has held at American universities. Twice dismissed as a student at Harvard, he has nevertheless the distinction of being a Fellow of the Royal Society of Arts of England and of the American Association for the Advancement of Science, and he has been honored by both the American Institute of Architects and the Royal Institute of British Architects—as well as by innumerable Awards of Merit, Grand Prizes, Gold Medals, and more than twenty-five honorary degrees.
Buckminster Fuller is the proto-typical universal man in an age of specialists. While on the one hand he appears to have originated in the Old Yankee tradition of inventive tinkering, he nevertheless preaches a doctrine of the messianic, international technological man and a scienfitic system called "synergetics."
Characteristically, "Bucky" is best described by himself: "Born in 1895, I have witnessed enough of the characteristics of acceleratingly-accelerating, evolutionary transformations and reorientation of humanity's know-what and know-how to be able to sense, think, and act fairly successfully, in realistic anticipation of epochally unfolding events."[23]

G. R. C.

16 Dirigible-delivered tower, comic strip   *(fig. 28)*

Mimeo-sketch (unique mimeographed copy of a sketch made on mimeograph stencil), 1927
Mimeograph ink on paper, 8 x 10" (20.3 x 26.4 cm.)
Unsigned
Lent by Ronald Feldman Fine Arts, New York City

"Projected delivery by zeppelin of the planned 10-deck, wirewheel, 4D tower apartment house. Fuller assumed that the dirigible, on approaching the site on which the house was to be erected, would throw out an anchor, then drop the bomb, creating by explosion the excavation to cradle the foundation. The 10-deck dwelling unit then would be lowered into the hole: the procedure, Fuller held, was 'like planting a tree.' The structure was to be supported by temporary stays until cement, poured about the base line, hardened."[24] The method of excavation can be compared with Hablik's *(fig. 9)* and the tower form with Frank Lloyd Wright's St. Mark's Tower.
When asked why he had used mimeograph, Fuller replied, "There was no other medium; I knew a friend who had a mimeograph machine. He let me use it at night. I found out that I could tear away the membrane and make the drawing come through much blacker and get some powerful results. It was a matter of economy."[25]

17 Hyperboloid housing towers, New York City, bird's-eye view   *(fig. 66)*

"Instant Slum Clearance: R. Buckminster Fuller designs a total solution to an American dilemma; here, for instance, is how it would work for Harlem: . . .
"Skyrise for Harlem is a proposal to rescue a quarter million lives by completely transforming their environment. New Harlem will encompass a half million people by removing old limits in exchange for natural boundaries. Harlem will widen from river to river across the island. Its new space will accommodate an additional quarter million residents— everyone willing to participate in the integrated transformation of a ghetto.
"Skyrise for Harlem can be completed in 36 months. The first year will be spent in what R. Buckminster describes as 'tooling up': organizing the mass production of structural parts and utility units, including all basic furniture. . . .

66.   *Fuller, Hyperboloid housing towers.* No. 17.

Rendering, November 1964
Pen and ink on tracing paper mounted on board, 21 x 24⅜" (53.4
x 61.4 cm.)
Signed: "Fuller and Sadao, Inc. Shoji Sadao"
Lent by Buckminster Fuller Archive, Philadelphia, Pennsylvania.

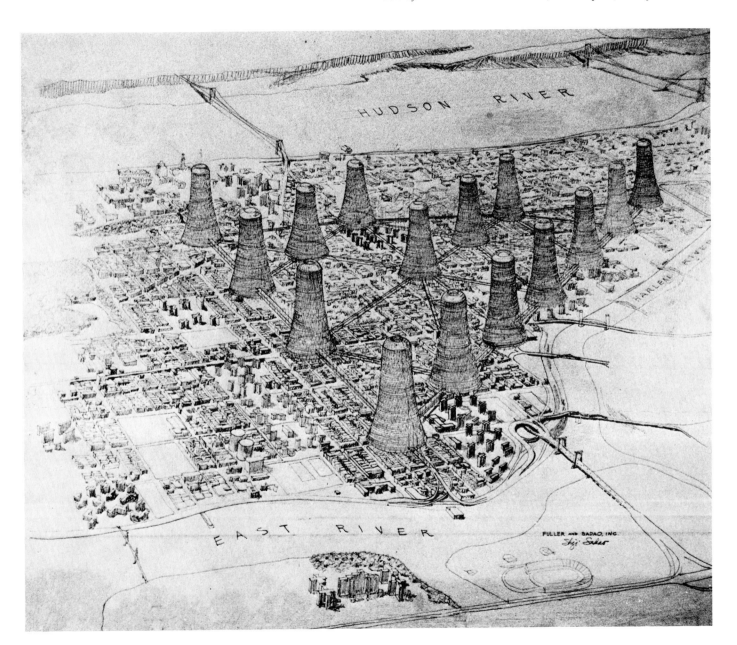

"An aerial view of New Harlem will disclose a radical landscape: vast, cleared ranges of space with fifteen peaks rising into the sky. These fifteen widely separated conical structures will house a half million people. A cross section of these structures resembles abstract, stylized Christmas trees evenly broadening toward their bases with central, supporting trunks. Each tree town is one hundred circular decks high. The lowest level begins ten stories aboveground, above dust level and major cloverleaf-highway systems. . . .
"A comprehensive designer must conserve natural resources and yet control their effects. One of Fuller's solutions for this design problem will be seen in the sky. Protective watersheds will enclose the sky of Harlem like overlapping umbrellas. Rain may cascade visibly from these watersheds to be piped into New York reservoirs. The watersheds float on the strength of transparent truss systems."[26]

18 "Triton City, a prototype floating community, 100,000 inhabitants, city plan"

Rendering, 1968
Pencil, ink, and zipatone on tracing paper, 27 x 37¾" (68.6 x 95.9 cm.)
Scale: 1" = 400'
Unsigned, rendered by Shoji Sadao
Lent by Fuller and Sadao, Inc.

19 "Triton City, Module 'A,' a prototype floating community, section" *(fig. 29)*

Rendering, 1968
Pencil, ink, and zipatone on tracing paper, 26⅝ x 36¾" (67.6 x 93.3 cm.)
Scale: 1" =32'
Unsigned, rendered by Shoji Sadao
Lent by Fuller and Sadao, Inc.

This study *(fig. 30)* was prepared by Triton Foundation, Inc. in 1968 under a grant from the U.S. Department of Housing and Urban Development to study the technical and economic feasibility of developing water areas immediately adjacent to the cores of major cities by floating entirely new communities.
The study was based on concepts of R. Buckminster Fuller, comprehensive designer and President of Triton Foundation

Inc. at that time. It was directed by Shoji Sadao, principal of Fuller and Sadao, Inc., and Peter Floyd, principal of Geometrics, Inc., both members of Triton Foundation. Over 80% of U.S. metropolitan areas with a population of 1,000,000 or more are near bodies of water sufficiently deep to accommodate such floating communities. Most have a depth adequate for shipping (25 to 30 feet) and relatively sheltered harbors. At these depths, a maximum average height of 20 stories can be floated.
The technology necessary to build floating cities is already in existence. Supertankers have been constructed which weigh 500,000 tons dead weight. The 5,000-person neighborhood module which was developed for this study is four acres in area and would weigh 150,000 tons. This basic unit would support an elementary school, a small supermarket, and local convenience stores and services. Three to six of these units, with a population of 15,000 to 30,000, would form a town. At this point a new town platform including a high school, more commercial, recreational, and civic facilities, and possibly some light industry could be added. When the community reaches the level of three to seven towns (90,000 to 125,000 population) it would become a full-scale city and would then add a city center module containing government offices, medical facilities, a shopping center, and possibly some form of special city-based activity such as a community college or specialized industry.
By designing a megastructure (i.e., an entire framework of structures and services) for high density residence, economies in transportation, services, and utilities can be realized. Preliminary cost estimates indicated that the whole fabric (including housing, schools, and other community facilities, all services, roads, and utilities) could be provided at a cost of $8,000 per person (at a density of 300 dwelling units per acre).

Shoji Sadao

The Historical Attempt by Man to
Convert His Evolution from a Subjective
to an Objective Process

from *No More Secondhand God and Other Writings* by
R. Buckminster Fuller

1.
The systematic growth
of man's intellectually-augmented evolution
is structured within
a progressively improved
scaffolding of assumptions.
The integrity of the principle
of intellectual assumptions
as bravely taken within the confines
of residual facts of disillusioned experience
is progressively persuasive.
For the new prospect of magnificent reality
looms into ken
as the retrospective lure of abandoned illusion
first dwarfs then dissolves.
Thereafter the temporary scaffolding
advantaged by informed appro::imation
of simplifying and interacting principles
is formally replaced by earned controls
consisting of ever more exact degrees
of measurement,
of the finitely interactive system,

of unique principles,
of energetic relationship,
of universe,
its inherent proclivities and articulations,
that is, its natural behavior.
The newly swollen growth
of total interaction of discovered,
equated, and valved-in principles
floods silently to contain
the subconscious rational of the
total individual—society.
Consciously, society is at first fascinated
by the novelties in technical manifestation
of the omnidirectional advance
as comparisoned only to the residual plurality
of fading traditional background illusions.
Wherefore:
ultimate social awareness
of total engulfment
by new orientation
to comprehensive principles of reality
appears first as enormous apprehension

of potential loss . . .
of what?
of things, of vanities,
of self-proclaimed prestige?
of the illusory values and
transitory standards and prerogatives
appropriate only to adjustments completed
in yesterdays diminutive gains,
by exceptional self?

2.
When man shall become preoccupied
with drawing off the progressive magnitudes
of new potential
to establish constant world-wide
advancement of living standards,
specifically: through the systematic incorporation
of scientific knowledge and technical advantage
in an earth-embracing service industry
of autonomous dwelling and intelligence
facility and felicity
insuring not only his progressive immunity
to annihilative factors of nature
but cohering his progressive appetite for truth
then will subside
the subjective requirements—
the negative motivations,
the antipathetic surges,
the concessions to survival-mandated compromise
promulgating the theory of
advancement by political initiative
whose expedient ways
are progressively powered by the
accumulating science and technology potential
to be tapped only for dubious war objectives.
It will take many waves
of threatened self-destruction
by society
to convince and instruct and
mobilize
an effectively articulate majority
of humanity
in the synchronization of society
towards an objective
evolutionary volition

inspired by deeply acknowledged faith
in an omniscient wisdom and benevolence
instructing through intellect . . .
(intellect wrote $e = mc^2$—
energy did not inscribe intellect $e = mc^2$)
intellect may write every
equation of physical behavior,
but no physical or abstract
equation will ever compass
intellect or its self-starter secret.

3.
When the objective evolution emerges
the intellectually architectured
house-of-tomorrow
will be central to the emergence.

Gropius, Walter (Berlin, 1883 — Boston, 1969)

From 1903 until 1907 Gropius studied architecture in Berlin and Munich. He worked as chief assistant in the Berlin office of Peter Behrens from 1907 until 1910, when he began his own architectural practice. From 1919 until 1928 he was director of the Bauhaus. Because of the National Socialists he left Germany in 1934, settling first in England where he had an office in partnership with Maxwell Fry. In 1937 he emigrated to the United States. He served as chairman of the Department of Architecture at Harvard's Graduate School of Design from 1938 until 1952. In 1946 he formed the Architects' Collaborative in Cambridge, Massachusetts, a large architectural firm which still exists.

20 "total theater," longitudinal section   *(fig. 14)*

Rendering, "1926"
Ink, watercolor, applied paper, 32¾ x 43" (83.2 x 109.2 cm.)
Lent by the Busch-Reisinger Museum, Harvard University, Cambridge, Massachusetts, Gift of Walter Gropius

21 Total Theater, plan   *(fig. 67)*

In 1926, Erwin Piscator, the Berlin stage director, contacted Gropius about the design of a theater. Piscator was known for his proletarian theater; he staged plays of immediate social concern, ones that he hoped would appeal to the disenfranchised, not just the middle class. As an extension of his political ideas concerning the theater, Piscator wanted to eliminate the traditional separation between actors and audience. To involve his audiences more directly with the play, he preferred a flexible stage, and he used scaffolds with movable stairs and elevators in the manner of the Russian Constructivist theater. Piscator also pioneered the use of projected photographs and films in place of fixed sets.[27] His intentionally unemotional approach, together with his interest in mechanical equipment to supplement human action, was very similar to the Neue Sachlichkeit phase of the Bauhaus.

The theater which Gropius designed for Piscator would have allowed for nearly total flexibility. It contained a center stage which, through the rotation of a large platform, could be turned into a proscenium; in addition, there was a more traditional deep stage. Two thousand seats were arranged as in an amphitheater, with no boxes. Sets could be augmented by projections onto twelve screens placed between the supporting columns of the structure, completely surrounding the spectators with those "sets." The stage platform was also designed so that it could be raised and lowered during performances. Although the architectural style of the Total Theater belongs to Gropius's International Style phase, in spirit it is indebted to Expressionist ideas of synaesthetic unity.[28]

The theater workshop at the Bauhaus, under the direction of Oskar Schlemmer, had been close to Piscator's conception of a unified theatrical production. Schlemmer's "Pantomime of Places," performed at the Bauhaus in 1924, used no conventional sets at all, only written signs announcing the "first crisis," the "second crisis," etc. Similarly, Laszlo

67. *Gropius, Total Theater.* No. 21.

Rendering, 1926
Ink, watercolor, applied paper, 30 x 40" (76.2 x 101.6 cm.)
Lent by the Busch-Reisinger Museum, Harvard University,
Cambridge, Massachusetts, Gift of Walter Gropius

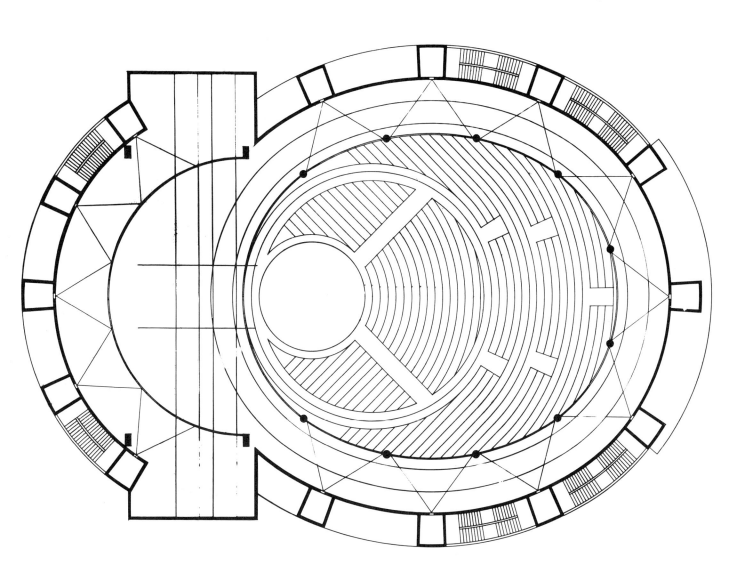

Moholy-Nagy's interests in combining human action with mechanical movements parallel those of Piscator. Moholy-Nagy's proposal of c. 1924 for the so-called "Mechanized Eccentric" called for three stages which included a projection screen for films and a place for mechanical instruments.[29] In the Total Theater Gropius wanted to create a theater "so impersonal that it never restrains [the producer] from giving his vision and imagination full play";[30] he wanted to attain the "mobilization of all three-dimensional means to shake off the audience's intellectually directed apathy, to overwhelm them, stun them, and force them to participate in experiencing the play."[31] As early as 1922 Gropius had seen theater as a manifestation of a transcendental[32] idea in whose realization the architect must assist through the creation of an imaginative realm, by using forms that, paradoxically, must not be too apparent and overwhelming. For Gropius the design of theaters at this time was not so much the external representation of cultural decorum, but was directed toward the creation of theatrical fantasy.[33]

Rosemarie Haag Bletter

Hablik, Wenzel August (Brüx, Bohemia, 1881—Itzehoe, Schleswig-Holstein, 1934)

Not a trained architect, Hablik was a painter, graphic artist, and designer active in the arts and crafts movement. He studied at the Kunstgewerbeschule des Österreichischen Museums in Vienna in 1904 and at the Malerakademie in Prague from 1905 to 1907. Hablik was subsequently awarded membership in Ferdinand Avenarious' Kunstwart Stiftung on the island of Sylt. His travels were limited to Greece and Turkey in 1910 and to South America in 1925-26. He settled in Itzehoe and in 1916 married Elizabeth Lindemann, a textile designer and weaver. Paintings of his were exhibited at the Berlin Sezession, 1909, the Deutscher Kunstlerbund in Weimar, 1910, and the Hagenbund Vereinigung in Vienna, 1911. His portfolio of etchings "Schaffende Kräfte" (1909) was shown at the third annual Sturm exhibition in 1912. Hablik was a member of the Arbeitsrat für Kunst founded in 1919 by Walter Gropius among others, and of Die Gläserne Kette (1919-1920) headed by Bruno Taut. Representative of Hablik's diverse interests are two later portfolios of etchings, "Das Meer" (1918) and "Cyklus Architektur" (1925). From 1927 on Hablik designed textiles for his wife's Werkstatt für Handweberei in Itzehoe, while continuing with his own work.

22 Der Bau der Luftkolonie (The Structure of a Colony-in-the-Air), overview   *(fig. 9)*

Sketch with marginalia, Wyk auf Föhr, December 29, 1908
Pencil on paper, glued to board, 8⅞ x 7⅛" (22.5 x 18 cm.)
Stamped: "Sammlung Hablik" (added by later archivist)
Lent by Susanne Klingeberg-Hablik, Itzehoe, Germany

This quick sketch was made during a vacation on one of the Frisian Islands in the North Sea. The airship makes a fleeting impression and yet it gains a certain specificity through the designations of interior and exterior parts. Hablik organized the air-colony into six multistoried polygonal capsules grouped around a central core and terminated by domes that carry cable-braced propeller systems.[34] The domes would contain machinery, baths, and storage facilities. Located beneath the utility domes, at varying levels, would be living, sleeping, and workshop spaces. On one of the lower levels small aircraft would be housed, each plane accommodating two to ten persons, undoubtedly for short excursions from the mother ship. The structure tapers to a conical tri-level network of arcaded promenades connected by elevators. Finally, at what is labeled the "diamond and metal point" of the base structure, Hablik imagined an "explosive anchor," a device (good for five successive uses) that would apparently excavate crater-like sites where the air-colony could land (cf. Fuller, *fig. 28*). Hablik almost certainly derived the unique form of the air-colony from his studies of crystal formations, which were a primary source of inspiration for architectural fantasies throughout his life.

23 Cyclus: Utopien, "fliegende siedlung" (Cycle: Utopias, "flying settlement"), panoramic view   *(fig. 68)*

Inscribed: *"technische Dinge sind niemals*
                          unmöglich/ so fern sie auf
                          Naturgesetzen aufgebaut sind.
                          Auch Naturgesetze waren einstmals
                          Utopien."

Conceived as part of a cycle of utopian images, this drawing of a flying settlement is a reinterpretation of the earlier colony-in-the-air as Hablik clearly acknowledged through his hyphenated dating—1907 (sic)/1914.[35] In this conception a long cylindrical core, tapered to points at each end, interpenetrates a drum-like volume. Cables secure the drum to the vertical core, and both of these sections are encircled by numerous propellers, those above the drum designated as part of the ship's steering mechanism. Atop the central core is a single propeller, while at the opposite end there is a rotating device that apparently is intended to give the vehicle the added flexibility of being able to touch down on water. Within the core would be located machinery, workshops, baths, and storerooms. The drum section would be comprised of two levels, the upper containing rooms for passengers, the lower consisting of a take-off and landing platform for small planes. The settlement and a smaller satellite hover high in the clouds above a distant city in the mountains.[36]

24 Berg-Dom. Bebaute Berge Spitzen.
   (Mountain Cathedral. Cultivated Mountain Peaks), panoramic view

Sketch with titling, 1920
Pen and ink on paper, mounted on board, 11¾ x 10½" (30.5 x 26.2 cm.)
Stamped: "Sammlung Hablik" and initialed with "20"
Lent by Susanne Klingeberg-Hablik, Itzehoe, Germany

Hablik created this vision of mountain-landscape architecture when he was involved with the utopian Expressionist group, Die Gläserne Kette. Prevalent in Expressionist circles was the idea that restructuring lofty mountain peaks into crystalline formations would create a paradisiacal ambience where awesome heights and the splendor of shimmering light would effect a spiritual awakening in those who journey there.[37] The association of crystals and crystalline effects with paradise and more generally with metaphysical forces in the universe may be traced back to ancient times. Hablik's thematic exploration of these ideas occurs in drawings of 1903 and in his little-known folio of 1909, "Schaffende Kräfte," so that the influence of Taut and other Expressionists upon him was certainly tempered by his own independent work of earlier date. In this drawing Hablik envisions an outburst of rocks, crystal spars, and jagged peaks at the foot of which is a succession of catch basins and mountain springs. Open, incomplete linear configurations at the base of the mountain establish broad planar areas, the slow angular rhythms of which give way to close-set triangular markings and flickering facets of light and shadow.[38]

25 Tower variation 3, "Cyklus: Ausstellungs—Bauten, Würfel, FLUSSPAT" (Cycle: Exhibition Building, Cube, FLUOR-SPAR), elevation from below   *(fig. 5)*

Drawing/watercolor, 1921
Pencil, watercolor, pen and ink on paper, 24⅜ x 18¾" (62.0 x 47.5 cm.)
Stamped: "Sammlung Hablik"
Lent by Susanne Klingeberg-Hablik, Itzehoe, Germany

During his association with the utopian Expressionists, Hablik began to use his studies of the geometry of crystals as a means of working out new designs for the tower archetype. The drawing is one of several variations in which he systematically derived forms based on the super-imposition and revolution of prismatic solids.[39] Rising from a polygonal base, this tower consists of four cubes of diminishing size that are rotated 45° to each other and are terminated by a polyhedric crystal. In similar drawings the tower is also an exhibition building, and its materials are listed as reinforced concrete, steel, and glass. The center of each side of the cubes has an elaborately framed entrance. Flanking these are large corner areas of glass and non-transparent rectilinear wall units. Like other drawings in the series, firm lines and contrasting color areas bring a precise hard-edged planarity to the tower image.[40] One imagines the tower as the focus of multitudes who journey from all cardinal points to be uplifted by the crystalline structure.

26 Zu dem Aufsatz: "Dombaugedanken." Jahrbuch: "Die Schopfung," Original Entwurf
(To the Superstructure: "Thoughts on the Construction of the Cathedral." Annual: "The Creation", original design), overview

Sketch with concentric phrasing and marginal diagrams, 1922
Pencil, ink, and watercolor on paper, 24⅞ x 18½" (65.0 x 50.1 cm.)
Stamped: "Sammlung Hablik"
Signed: "W. A. Hablik, Itzehoe" in pencil
Lent by Susanne Klingeberg-Hablik, Itzehoe, Germany
Inscribed: *"Dom im offenden Meer, so gross dass die Schiffe den "Weltsonntag" darin feiern können.*

Über alles hinweg schwingt sich der Geist!
(Siehe freitragende Kuppel)

68.   *Hablik, Flying Settlement. No. 23.*

Elaborated sketch, 1907/1914
Pen and ink and colored pencil on tracing paper, glued to board, 14
x 14⅝" (35.5 x 37.4 cm.)
Stamped: "Sammlung Hablik"
Lent by Susanne Klingeberg-Hablik, Itzehoe, Germany

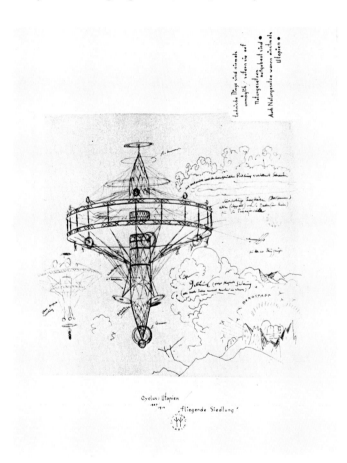

Denkt an ganz grosse Aufgaben!
Denkt an eine neue Religion!
Denkt an Natur und ihre Wunder!"

The domical building was a recurrent theme in Hablik's
work. His designs for domical structures recall late
eighteenth-century projects by the Romantic Classicists—
for example Boullée's Cenotaph to Sir Isaac Newton. The
cathedral-in-the-sea is composed of a high central domical
space from which radiate low, covered passageways for ships
that alternate with open basins and are ringed by a unifying
arcade.[41] The dome rises from a double-tiered drum to carry
a profusion of aerials. Placed at the lower edge of the drawing
are two pencil sketches which are the result of Hablik's
crystallographic studies and suggest that the dome's structure
would be a system of superimposed trusses. The "free-
standing dome" of the cathedral relates to a series of similar
projects.[42] Manifest in the drawing is a lightness of line and a
tight working of circular and radial configurations. Arching
loosely around the image are notations in which Hablik
expands upon the cosmic symbolism of the project:
"Cathedral in the open sea, so large that ships can celebrate
'world Sunday' in it. Above all vibrates a Spirit!. . . Think
about great superior tasks! Think about a new religion!
Think about Nature and its wonder!"[43]

Eugene A. Santomasso

Herron, Ron (London, 1930-)

*A less verbal member of Archigram, Ron Herron's superb drawings
convey some of the most striking of the group's images. He is a
magnificent draughtsman, producing drawings remarkable for their
visual impact, even on the distractingly chaotic pages of Archigram
publications.*

*Herron first became involved with Archigram in 1961 when Peter
Cook approached him for contributions to Archigram I. At the time
he and Warren Chalk were both working at the London County
Council Schools Division. The two of them became frequent
contributors to Archigram pages. The entire Archigram group,
including Herron, worked with Theo Crosby in 1962 on a plan for
the redevelopment of Euston Station, and in 1963 Herron, Cook et
al. organized and built Archigram's "Living City" exhibition.
Herron and Crosby are now partners in the design firm, Pentagram.
Herron lives in London, is married and has two children.*

27 Cities: Moving; Master Vehicle—
Habitation 1964/4, elevation   *(fig. 69)*

The "master vehicle" shown here is only one of several units
of the Walking City. The City is composed of an indefinite
number of such units, each containing different urban areas
and residential districts, and all linked by retractable
corridors. These containers with controlled micro-climates
and retractable sun-roofs stalk about the landscape, grouping
and regrouping at will.

The obvious question, of course: "Is he serious? Can Herron
really expect us to live in these crawling bug-faced
carapaces?" No, not really. He's having fun drawing his
fantastic creations. But at the same time, the Walking City is
an expression in architectural terms, albeit ironic ones, of the
Archigram vision of society. The social structure of cities is
not static; mobility, flexibility, and change are the dominant
characteristics of modern urban life. Our cities are, in fact,
moving—the average household moves once every three
years. If they lived in Ron Herron's "Cities: Moving" they
wouldn't even have to pack.

Janet White

69. *Herron, Walking Cities. No. 27.*

Orthographic rendering, November, 1964
Ink on paper, 22 x 33″ (55.8 x 83.8 cm.)
Labeled: "November 1964, Ron Herron"
Lent by Gilman Paper Co.

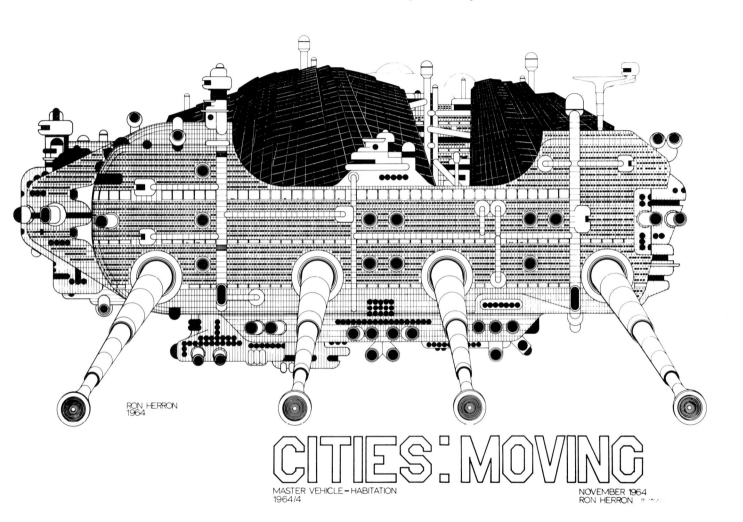

RON HERRON
1964

CITIES: MOVING

MASTER VEHICLE – HABITATION
1964/4

NOVEMBER 1964
RON HERRON

Hollein, Hans (Vienna, 1934-)

Hans Hollein studied architecture at the Academy of Fine Arts in Vienna, where he received his diploma in 1956. Between 1955 and 1958, while working in an architectural firm in Sweden, he published his early ideas on an absolute architecture and created his first architectural projects. He then came to the United States where he studied at the Illinois Institute of Technology and the University of California at Berkeley, receiving his Master of Architecture at Berkeley in 1960.

Since his return to Vienna that same year he has participated in various conferences and in exhibitions in Stockholm, Berlin, Rome, Venice, and elsewhere; he has taught as a Visiting Professor at Washington University in St. Louis (1963-64); he has established his own practice in Vienna (1964); and he has continued to publish his ideas, to design visionary architecture, and to construct buildings and sculpture. His most ambitious recent projects include the Museum of Modern Art in Florence and the Municipal Museum in Monchengladbach, Germany, both begun in the mid-seventies. Among the several prizes received by him are the Reynolds Memorial Award for the Retti Candleshop in Vienna (1966), The Austrian State Award for Environmental Design (1968), and the Prize of the City of Vienna (1974).

New Yorkers may see an example of his work at 27 East 79th Street in the renovated facade of the Hanae Mori Boutique (formerly Feigen Gallery).

28 High-rise Building; Sparkplug Project, perspective *(fig. 40)*

Rendering, 1964
Photomontage, 4¾ x 7¼ " (12 x 18.4 cm.)
Lent by the Museum of Modern Art, New York City, Philip Johnson Fund

In this drawing, the reproduction of the sparkplug is in newsprint form. It has been trimmed as close to its outer boundaries as possible and then glued directly onto a photograph of a gently undulating, European prairie landscape. Clusters of trees and several farm buildings

Rendering, 1964
Photomontage, 4¾ x 14½" (12 x 36.8 cm.)
*Lent by the Museum of Modern Art, New York City, Philip
Johnson Fund*

punctuate the landscape, which is largely cultivated, and an
open sky serves as a backdrop for the towering sparkplug.
Formally, Hollein owes much to the Dada movement: his
high-rise is really a two-dimensional, photomontage "found
object" which has been inserted into a new context and
endowed with a new meaning, as were the actual found
objects such as a bicycle wheel or a latrine which Dadaist
Marcel Duchamp elevated to the level of Art by placing them
on a pedestal.

But the changed scale of the sparkplug vis-à-vis the houses in
the landscape suggests the influence of sculptor Claes
Oldenburg. Making preliminary sketches primarily in
watercolor and ink, Oldenburg has depicted countless

over-sized objects, whether up-ended scissors or melting Good Humor bars in cityscapes or stretches of countryside. But while Oldenburg's fantasies are usually whimsical and light, those of Hollein are ironic, hard and often rather frightening. In the hands of both men, however, the ordinary becomes monumentalized.

29 Carrier-City in Landscape Project, aerial perspective   *(fig. 70)*

Again a newsprint reproduction (now of the U.S.S. *Enterprise*) has been glued onto the photograph of a partially cultivated rural landscape. So panoramic is the view of the hollows and hills, however, that two separate photographs are needed in order to include all of it. But the two photographs have been juxtaposed carefully and the cutout of the aircraft carrier has been glued over the seam as if in an attempt to conceal it. As the section reveals, the hull of the *Enterprise* is meant to appear buried in the earth, the flight deck flush with the earth's surface and the bridge rising above it like a watchtower. Thus, the aircraft carrier becomes an underground city set in arcadian surroundings, its flight deck serving as both roof and "piazza."[44]
Like the sparkplug, the carrier is utterly out of context. But unlike the sparkplug, it is not forbiddingly surreal, for it does not lack windows and doors; nor has it been blown up to an unnatural size. In short, it is already a piece of architecture, both human in scale and inhabitable.
Because the temperature of the earth is relatively even beneath its surface, builders have turned to underground construction in recent years so that their structures can be heated and cooled economically. Therefore, even though Hollein's vision has not been imitated in its form by contemporary designers, his notion of a sunken architecture has become a modern, functional reality.

30 Carrier-City in Landscape Project, section   *(fig. 54)*

Rendering, 1964.
Photomontage, 6⅜ x 15⅜" (15.5 x 39.2 cm.)
Lent by the Museum of Modern Art, New York City, Philip Johnson Fund

Pen and ink draughtsmanship complements the photomontage technique in this drawing which shows the U.S.S. *Enterprise* in cross section. But rather than use a newsprint reproduction of the aircraft carrier, Hollein here uses a glossy photograph, again trimmed along the outer edge of the vessel's form. And the landscape is not photographed, as in the other two renderings; rather, it is sketched onto the glazed paper support with black ink, delicately rippling lines describing the terrain above ground, ruler-straight, diagonal hatchings representing the earth beneath the surface.
Not included in the exhibition is another composition in the aircraft carrier series which shows the ship resting in the landscape on its keel, the dark undersides of its hull looming eerily above the viewer. A copy of this version is owned by Claes Oldenburg.

Mary D. Edwards

Isozaki, Arata (Oita City, Japan, 1931-)

Arata Isozaki studied architecture at Tokyo University, earning a baccalaureate in 1954 and a doctorate in 1961. From 1953 to 1963 he worked with Kenzo Tange's Team and URTEC[45] on such projects as the 1960 Tokyo Plan. In 1963 he established his own firm. Isozaki was not a member of the Metabolist Group, but his own work of the early 1960s reflects his involvement with Metabolist ideas. However, where Metabolist design methodology frequently gives precedence to technological solutions at the expense of form, Isozaki holds form and drama as essential architectural elements. A fascination with the manipulation of simple geometric forms characterizes much of his work (Nakayama House, 1964; Shuku-sha Building, 1975), and his buildings are rich in quotations and allusions to a variety of architects and images, mostly of western origin. The Fujimi Country Club House in Oita (1972-74), for example, draws directly on Palladio and Ledoux. Isozaki's efforts to create symbiotic relationships between form and technology, East and West, and present and past have made him a central figure in Post-Metabolist thought.

31 "Spatial Construction," orthographic elevation   *(fig. 60)*

Rendering, 1960
Ink on photographic reproduction, 14⅞ x 31″ (37.3 x 78.7 cm.)
Signed: " '60 Arata Isozaki"
Lent by Arata Isozaki

In this process drawing Isozaki has added transportation elements to his already rendered megastructure of shafts and trusses. He prepared the proposal in 1960 while employed by Kenzo Tange's Team. Unlike the truss structures appearing in Tange's 1960 Tokyo Plan, which have square shafts that limit future growth to only four possible directions, Isozaki's round shafts allow expansion in any direction. They also have an evocative quality absent in the Tokyo Plan structures. The roughly textured shafts supporting beams recall ancient post and lintel construction; Isozaki made this association clear in another study by combining a drawing of his structure with photographs of Greek columns.

32 "Trees become Forest," elevations   *(fig. 44)*

Sketchbook page, 1960-62
Pen and ink on paper, 10⅛ x 7¼″ (26 x 18.5 cm.)
Unsigned
Lent by Arata Isozaki

33 "Clusters in the Air," elevation

Sketchbook page, 1960-62
Pen and ink on paper, 7¼ x 10⅛″ (18.5 x 26 cm.)
Unsigned
Lent by Arata Isozaki

34 "Clusters in the Air," elevation   *(fig. 45)*

Sketchbook page, 1960-62
Pen and ink on paper, 7¼ x 10⅛″ (18.5 x 26 cm.)
Unsigned
Lent by Arata Isozaki

Isozaki worked independently from 1960 to 1962 on his project "Clusters in the Air." The idea is an outgrowth of the slightly earlier "Spatial Construction." In both schemes Isozaki created artificial land high above ground level permitting construction of a new Metabolist city without first demolishing the old city, but the individual structures of the cluster city are more independent, structurally and aesthetically, than those of the "Spatial Construction."

The final model for the "Clusters in the Air" has received considerable attention because the structures have some resemblance to the system of brackets projecting from a central post used to support the broad roofs of traditional Japanese temples. The three drawings shown here suggest that this was not the only image Isozaki had in mind. The sketch, "Trees Become Forest," illustrates a situation in nature that parallels the one Isozaki wished to create in the city. Each tree in a young forest stands as a self-sufficient entity, but as the forest matures, the branches of neighboring trees eventually touch and intertwine, creating a zone of life above the ground. Isozaki's two studies of clusters show the individual structures linking up like the trees in the forest, the traffic and buildings below them may be compared to the smaller plants on the forest floor.

The "Clusters in the Air" are neither a forest nor colossal parts of temple roofs but the synthesis of a number of elements including the system of forest growth and certain concepts underlying temple construction. Isozaki's project does not refer obsequiously back to Japan's past as much as it incorporates viable principles into an architecture that is truly of the present.

35 Studies for Tokyo Central District, 2 elevations

Sketchbook page, 1962-63
Red and black ballpoint pen on paper, 10⅛ x 7¼"
(26 x 18.5 cm.)
Unsigned
Lent by Arata Isozaki

36 Studies for Tokyo Central District, plan

Sketchbook page, "3/jan. 63."
Black, blue, and red ballpoint pen on paper mounted on board, 10⅛ x 7¼" (26 x 18.5 cm.)
Unsigned
Lent by Arata Isozaki

Isozaki continued his work on schemes for elevated cities in his 1962 and 1963 studies for Tokyo's central district. The forms of the individual structures vary from drawing to drawing, but in all cases they have been subordinated to the continuity of the frame connecting them. The frame represented in these drawings follows the existing street grid. At this stage Isozaki does not appear to be interested in the architectural qualities of the project as much as the general relationship between the new city and the old city and the flow of traffic.

37 "Hiroshima . . . ," overview *(fig. 71)*

Study for the Electric Labyrinth (for the 14th Triennale in Milan, 1968): on a giant photomural of Hiroshima as it looked shortly after its destruction by the atomic bomb Isozaki projected changing images such as the ruined megastructures seen in this photo collage. Ruins provide an important metaphor for Isozaki's work. "Ruins are dead architecture. Their total image has been lost. The remaining fragments require the operation of the imagination if they are to be restored. Anything that is done to them after they have become ruins is limited to replacement of lost parts with new ones. At the instant when perfect saturation—complete restoration—has been attained, the ruins face the oncome of another void and reversion to the ruined state. Within a time that imposes these conditions, ruins inevitably confront corrosion."[46]

Richard Cleary

71.   *Isozaki, Hiroshima* ... No. 37.

Photomontage, 1968
Collage of photographs, 14 x 37" (35.6 x 94.0 cm.)
Signed: "Arata Isozaki '68"
Lent by Arata Isozaki

Kahn, Louis I. (Island of Saarama, Russia, 1901—New York City, 1974)

Kahn received his architectural education in the early 1920s at the University of Pennsylvania, a bastion of Beaux Arts method, under Paul Cret. A gifted draughtsman, he worked after his graduation in a series of Philadelphia offices; in the mid-1930s and 1940s he was associated with the emigré architects Alfred Kastner and, later, Oscar Stonorov (as well as with George Howe), who introduced him to the ideas of the European modernists. Much of his work during these years was concerned with housing and city planning projects. Kahn did not emerge as a major figure until the early 1950s, but since this time his influence as a designer, teacher, and poet-philosopher of architectural theory has been immense. His mature work combines the reappearance of Beaux Arts elements of monumentality, symmetry, and geometric planning and massing with a metaphysical conception of "what a building wants to be." In providing an expressive alternative to the dominant International Style aesthetic, Kahn became a prophet and hero for the generation of American architects schooled in the 1950s and 1960s.

Carol Willis

38 City Tower, structural study, plan
1953-57
Pencil and colored pencil on tracing paper, 11 ⅞ x 9¾" (30.2 x 24.8 cm.)
Unsigned. Drawn by Anne Griswold Tyng
Lent by Kahn Archive, Philadelphia, Pennsylvania

39 City Tower, study of sunshades *(brises soleils),* elevation   *(fig. 72)*

Anne Griswold Tyng was the associated architect in this "exploration into the nature of a high-rise structure."
"The challenge . . . is to evolve more meaningful form out of the nature of high-rising structure. This form must express: the buttress to wind forces which tend to topple it . . . the cumulative force of weight tending to crush its base . . . a logical balance between services and usable space . . . variety in floor area and ceiling height to accommodate various functions. . . ."
A concept of natural growth:
"In Gothic times, architects built in solid stones. Now we can build with hollow stones. The spaces defined by the members of a structure are as important as the members. These spaces range in scale from the voids of an insulation panel, voids for air, lighting and heat to circulate, to spaces big enough to walk through or live in.
"The desire to express voids positively in the design of the structure is evidenced by the growing interest and work in the development of space frames. The forms being experimented with come from a closer knowledge of nature and the outgrowth of the constant search for order. Design habits leading to the concealment of structure have no place in this implied order. Such habits retard the development of an art. I believe that in architecture, as in all art, the artist instinctively keeps the marks which reveal how a thing was done. The feeling that our present day architecture needs embellishment stems in part from our tendency to fair joints out of sight, to conceal how parts are put together. Structures should be devised which can harbor the mechanical needs of rooms and spaces. Ceilings with structure furred in tend to erase scale. If we were to train ourselves to draw as we build, from the bottom up, when we do, stopping our pencil to make a mark at the joints of pouring or erecting, ornament would grow out of our love for the expression of method. It would follow that the pasting over the construction of lighting and acoustical material, the burying of tortured

1953-57
Pen and ink on paper, 17 ⅜ x 13 ⅝" (43.8 x 34.6 cm.)
Unsigned. Drawn by Louis I. Kahn
Lent by Kahn Archive, Philadelphia, Pennsylvania

unwanted ducts, conduits and pipe lines, would become intolerable. The desire to express how it is done would filter through the entire society of building, to architect, engineer, builder and craftsman."

Louis I. Kahn[47]

40 Philadelphia, Penn Center project, perspective

Study sketch, 1956-57?
Pencil on tracing paper, 11 ¾ x 15 ⅛" (29.8 x 38.4 cm.)
Unsigned
Lent by Toshio Nakamura, Tokyo

41 Philadelphia, Penn Center project, perspective with City Tower (Cf. nos. 38, 39)   *(fig. 22)*

Study sketch, 1956-57?
Charcoal on tracing paper, 11 x 15 ⅜" (27.9 x 38.5 cm.)
Inscribed: "L. Kahn"
Lent by Toshio Nakamura, Tokyo

These two small but mighty drawings record two phases of Kahn's Project for Market Street East, of 1956-57. The first (no. 40), dating from 1956, shows us a vast plaza, defined along its north side by a hedge of sternly monumental building masses. The scale tends toward the awesome; the drawing is bold, the lines thick, almost savage. The enormous plaza is in two levels, but its major plane rushes uncompromisingly toward City Hall, and in this drawing Kahn subordinates the kiosk-like shelters which were intended to populate it in order to open it up visually and to increase its velocity: a setting for heroes, but still fundamentally Ville Radieuse in conception.
In the second drawing of 1957 *(fig. 22)*, Kahn diminishes the dominance of that main east-west plaza space by making it seem narrower and by interrupting it in various ways. He also breaks down the military front along the north side by eliminating the most aggressively cubical of his buildings in order to open out a wide cross axis leading into the richly textured dark mass of the major marketing center, "the cathedral of the city." It is a great animal, a sphinx of a building. Beyond it Kahn's and Anne Tyng's new space-frame skyscraper project, of 1957, now proudly dances, stepping forward in the space. The whole drawing sways and shimmers from light to dark with a kind of joyful physicality which is lacking in the first, a rather stiff if grandly austere drawing. The second is atmospheric, passionate, and full of movement, at once more human and more original to Kahn. Indeed, between the two drawings Kahn moved from a classicizing geometry of closed masses and vast voids in the first to a more personal, more romantic interweaving of buildings and spaces in the second. Throughout his life Kahn's design was to be pulled back and forth, seeking an equilibrium between those poles.

Vincent Scully

Kiesler, Frederick J. (Vienna, 1896—New York City, 1965)

Architect and sculptor, Kiesler dedicated his life to the primacy of the organic over the technological, and from the time he abandoned business school for art school pursued the curvilinear and continuous in design, often in the most non-conformist ways. He worked with Adolf Loos and the Dutch de Stijl group before immigrating to the U.S.A. in 1926 at the invitation of the Theatre Guild and the Little Review. *He was scenic director for the Juilliard School of Music from 1933 to 1957 and managed a design laboratory at the Columbia University School of Architecture from 1936 to 1942. He designed many theater productions and with Armand Bartos built the World House Gallery in New York (1957) and the Shrine of the Book in Jerusalem (1959).*

G. R. C.

Kiesler's drawings reveal the hand of a classically-trained artist as well as an architect. They are spontaneous, organic, and energetic, showing a variety and intensity that suggest a relationship between the quality of his line and his vision.
"... I saw Kiesler do something that astonished me. He took his index finger and moved it around from right to left in space, and then made an outline in the air, going slightly up and slightly down... As I learned later this movement solved a problem of the auditorium for the new theater he's designing for the Ford Foundation. He was actually guiding his body by his finger through the auditorium... He actually experiences architecture with his body, through his physical senses, and not through any theoretical or abstract notion of architecture. Perhaps this is why his drawings have immediacy..."[48]
Whether in air or on paper, Kiesler used drawing as a way to study a problem. In the act of drawing, design solutions were found. His drawings are loose and spontaneous because they record the immediacy of the working process.
"... the pencil touches the empty paper of the pad;... I start to scribble, truly scribble. There is no intention or inner desire to produce draftsmanship. Yet I cannot say that it is automatic writing or designing. It is play—a deliberate playing with pencil and paper—and there is continuous reading of the gradually evolving designs... I deliberately detach myself from it, as soon as an answer is indicated. Not yet given. But indicated. Strange, it seems I shun an ultimate solution. As a cat postpones the kill of the mouse. There is lust in his postponement."[49]

42 Endless House: elevation showing staircase, window openings in shell, living room   *(fig. 73)*

43 Endless House: spiral shell construction   *(fig. 23)*

Sketch, 1959
Ink on block paper, 5 x 9" (13 x 23 cm.)
Unsigned
Lent by André Emmerich Gallery, New York City

44 Endless House: Outlooks No. 1, elevation   *(fig. 49)*

Sketch, 1959
Pencil on block paper, 8¼ x 11¾" (21 x 30 cm.)
Initialed
Lent by André Emmerich Gallery, New York City

45 Endless House: "sleeping" and "dressing" area

Sketch, 1959
Ink on block paper, 8¼ x 11⅝" (21 x 29.5 cm.)
Initialed
Lent by André Emmerich Gallery, New York City

The "Endless," be it house, theater, or museum, in the shape
of an egg, a shell, a cave, or a whale, was the visionary plan of
Frederick Kiesler.
"A big wave rolled over the land from the sea and flooded all
concrete columns and colonnades and they collapsed like
sand, disintegrating like bubbles. And the people were
without roofs. Without roofs over their heads, they almost
lost their minds. But unexpectedly the big wave set a magic
eggshell ashore. And it rolled. The fire couldn't catch it,
and on the flood it swam. No beam, no column made its
structure, yet a roof and a wall and a floor were all there.
In a day.[50]

The Endless House was to be made of reinforced concrete
molded into a double-curved shell-form, the resulting dome
to act as a combined structural and space enclosing element
in which the loads of compression and tension were equalized
all along its spherical pre-stressed skin. It could enclose any
irregularly shaped area with a single structural element,
thereby escaping the limitations of a circular, square, or
rectangular plan. With curved walls and unrestricted interior
space, the dweller was free to enclose or open spaces and to
alter their uses as needed. "The 'Endless House' is indeed a
very practical house if one defines practicality in not too
narrow a sense, and if one considers the poetry of life an
integral part of everyday happenings."[51] First designed in
1923-24 and later adapted for a furniture showroom in 1933,
the Endless House was never built as a house. Two models
were shown publicly, one to house a David Hare sculpture for
an exhibition at the Kootz Gallery in 1950 and the other for
the Museum of Modern Art (*fig. 24*). The latter was intended
as a model for a full-size Endless to be erected in the MOMA
sculpture garden in the early 1960s, a plan never realized
because of the museum's building expansion.

"The 'Endless' is finite as to mechanics, and definite in its
destruction of boundaries between areas of eating, sleeping,
playing; between outside and inside, strangers and home
folks. Privacy can be produced in any section of the 'Endless'

and continuity of space as well. Swinging wall sections,
folding, rolling, fanning overhead or sidewise—that's a
cinch in our ball-bearing age, space on pivots and time on
coasters . . . The strait jackets are burst. Life has a chance to
become inventive. You, as the inhabitant, then become the
real architect of your house."[52]

46 Universal Theater, front elevation

Rendering, 1960-61
Ink on tracing paper, 12⅛ x 29¾" (43.5 x 75.5 cm.)
Scale ⅛" = 1'
Stamped
Lent by André Emmerich Gallery, New York City

47 Universal Theater, plan and section

Rendering, 1960-61
Pencil on paper, 18⅛ x 26" (46 x 66 cm.)
Unsigned
Lent by André Emmerich Gallery, New York City

"THE THEATRE IS DEAD.

WE ARE NOT WORKING FOR NEW
DECORATION.
WE ARE NOT WORKING FOR NEW LITERATURE.
WE ARE NOT WORKING FOR NEW LIGHTING
SYSTEMS.
WE ARE NOT WORKING FOR NEW MASKS.
WE ARE NOT WORKING FOR NEW COSTUMES.
WE ARE NOT WORKING FOR NEW ACTORS.
WE ARE NOT WORKING FOR NEW THEATRES.
WE ARE WORKING FOR THE THEATRE THAT
HAS SURVIVED THE THEATRE.
WE ARE WORKING FOR THE SOUND BODY OF A
NEW SOCIETY.
AND WE HAVE CONFIDENCE IN THE STRENGTH
OF NEWER GENERATIONS.
THAT ARE AWARE OF THEIR PROBLEMS.

THE THEATRE IS DEAD.
WE WANT TO GIVE IT A SPLENDID BURIAL.
ADMISSION 75 CENTS."[53]

Sketch, "September 14/58" Chicago
Blue ink on block paper, 8¼ x 11¾" (21 x 30 cm.)
Initialed
Lent by André Emmerich Gallery, New York City

The Endless Theater was designed as a "stadium for the people," a multi-purpose space "encompassing the world of theater in a single concept."[54] Its many stages, tracks, and continuous runways, interwoven with rings of spectator seats at various levels, made the audience part of the show. "Actors themselves no longer interest us. The new movement in the theater includes all the people. Audiences now are cramped and grow tired before the play is over. In the new theater they will move about at will, take part in the play if they so desire and stay as long as they please for the program will be continuous."[55]

The stage was to be transformed from the traditional proscenium design into a funnel-shaped enclosure with floor raised to mount gradually back, side wings closed in recession and overhead gently inclined toward the front. By tipping the axis of the stage, which would allow the audience to see the ground plan of the set, Kiesler enabled the spectator to translate the dramatic action into correct spatial distancing and thereby place himself in a physical relationship to it. Further to enhance this effect, there was to be no curtain, and no darkening of house lights in lieu of a curtain. Performances were to be continuous with no interruptions from beginning to end, and all entrances and exits of actors were to be left fully visible.

The Endless Theater later became part of the Universal Theater, a multi-purpose art/industrial/business complex that Kiesler developed to save theater from what he saw as an isolation that threatened its survival. First designed in 1932, it was expanded in 1961 for the Ford Foundation "Ideal Theater" project. Again, the theater was a shell structure designed as a flexible container, with possibility for wide variations of sound, light, and stage action.

Janet Kaplan

Kikutake, Kiyonori (Kyushu, 1928-)

Kikutake received his Bachelor of Architecture at Waseda University in 1950 and established his own office three years later. He had an early interest in what is now called "recycling" and was occupied with such projects in Kyoto and Osaka. His own residence in Tokyo, the Sky House of 1958, was designed with replaceable units and certainly led to his interest in this aspect of Metabolist theory.

It was in 1958 that he envisioned the tower-shaped community that we exhibit, with its clip-on cylindrical living units that allow for change and replacement. In 1958 he also designed his first Marine City, a concept that he has pursued down to the present. He worked out a model of such a floating-platform structure with American engineers for Hawaii in 1971, constructed a modest-sized one for the Okinawa exhibition of 1975, is currently working on the practical details of a floating city in collaboration with the engineer Masanobu Shinozuka of Columbia University, and has been asked this year to advise on a floating hotel off Atlantic City, New Jersey. Of the several young architects who made up the Metabolist group in Japan in 1960 and are now among the major practicing architects of Japan, Kikutake is perhaps the most "engineering" in character although his ultimate interests are clearly to use science to the benefit of humaity, i.e., "Metabolism."

Kikutake has won many competitions, he has received many awards, and he has lectured or taught in many countries. He is a visionary architect whose dreams have been built.

The projects for Marine City and Tower Shaped City, sketched in 1958, were published in 1959 in Kokusai Kenchiku *(International Architecture). During the next five years the separate projects were themselves combined, producing the Marine City of 1963. The original schemes were also published at length—with many of our drawings as illustrations—in the famous manifesto of the group:* Metabolism/1960: The Proposals for New Urbanism, *which carried statements by Kikutake, Kawazoe, Maki/Ohtaka, and Kurokawa, initiators of the movement.*

48 Tower Shaped City, overlay sections with marginals *(fig. 74)*

49 Tower Shaped City, elevation *(fig. 55)*

Preparation for rendering,1958
Red pencil on tracing paper, 32¾ x 20¼" (83 x 51.5 cm.)
Signed: "K. Kikutake, 1 Nov. 1958"
Lent by Kiyonori Kikutake

50 Tower Shaped City and Marine City, perspective panorama *(fig. 48)*

Preparation for rendering
Photograph of no. 49 collaged onto a penciled panoramic landscape of Japan, 16½ x 17" (42 x 43.5 cm.)
Signed: "K. Kikutake 11 Feb. 1959"
Lent by Kiyonori Kikutake

As can be seen, the study was worked out in section (no. 48), then the tower drawn in detail (no. 49), photographed, and mounted on a pencil sketch of its setting on Sagami Bay off Tokyo. The steps in the procedure were as follows: (process of montage): 1) basic drawing stating the dimensions; 2) adding the outline of the entire dwelling units; 3) shading with color pencils producing the three-dimensional effect; 4) making the basic layout using the format required for the magazine publication; 5) printing the drawing in the ratio calculated from the basic drawing; 6) sticking the printed photograph in its place; 7) finishing the drawing according to the basic drawing.

Kikutake wrote about the project: "City planning must be planning for the future, and it must be based on ambition and imagination for the future.

"The megapolis of Tokyo is now tired and sick. Not only has that mammoth city lost its control as a city, it is even trying to conceal and justify the facts of its own illness by relying upon the adaptability of the 8,000,000 people who live there.

"The life environment in such a 'horizontal city' not only has deteriorated far beyond transportation capacities and limits of inhabitability but has also become hopelessly overcrowded. A cancerous and harmful tissue is covering the city, and is beginning to turn to the suburban residential areas as well. . . .

"The tower city is a proposal to solve the problem of 'living' generally, intensively, and urbanely....

"With the adoption of this tower city, it is anticipated that the question of population per hectare may be solved on the basis of from 1,000 to 1,500 people per hectare, but the aim of the proposal is not to increase the population density. Rather, the idea of the tower city is proposed as an effective way to revitalize existing cities and as a public project to create a better living environment. It also indicates how important it is for a city to be prepared in a planned and general way and how necessary the accumulation of technology is....

"The tower will have a structure capable of supporting 1,250 family units, and its dynamic shape overflowing with strength will not merely symbolize one function but will also be a total expression of real support for people's life, with the inside of its wall filled with all necessary public utility systems, like the tissues of a tree trunk.

"A production facilities plant will be built in the tower to construct the whole structure gradually from the lower part to the upper part. First, a concrete tower will be built to serve as the trunk structure. The necessary parts will be manufactured inside the tower to be added in the same way as silkworms build their cocoons by spinning from their own mouths.

"After the concrete trunk structure is completed, the plant will be immediately switched over to become a factory for the manufacture of housing units. The factory will now produce not concrete materials but steel goods. All the 1,250 housing units will be assembled at this factory and installed on the tower....

"Traffic will be vertical, adding no additional burden to the existing horizontal traffic system and facilitating the smooth flow of transportation inside the tower. In the field of transportation, families living on the 20th floor will be in almost the same situation as those on the lower 10 floors, thus preventing unnecessary traffic confusion....

"As a tree puts forth buds, grows leaves, puts on autumnal tints, and loses its leaves according to the natural order of the four seasons, so will a housing unit share its life cycle with the family living in it....

"It is necessary that the relation between man and architecture go beyond a physical relationship and be strengthened by a new spiritual factor. Moreover, Japanese architecture shows that such is possible.

"This was once evident in the Ise and Izumo shrines and Horyuju Temple, but, I think, has been already forgotten because of the buildings' relations with religion. A feeling of tension in space is created by the low "kondo" (main hall of the temple) and the high-rising five-story pagoda set in the corridor-surrounded compounds of Horyuji Temple and the plot of Ise Shrine, seemingly polished right in the midst of a natural scene of green seas; these intense impressions are certainly the result of design."[56]

51 Nova Block housing for Marine City, elevation

Study sketch, 1960
Ink on tracing paper, 22½ x 23" (57 x 58.5 cm.)
Signed: "K. Kikutake"
Lent by Kiyonori Kikutake

52 Nova Block housing for the Marine City, working system

Overlay study sketches, 1960
Pencil and marker on tracing paper, mounted on cardboard, 15¾ x 10⅞" (40 x 27.5 cm.)
Signed: "K. Kikutake, 22 March 1960"
Lent by Kiyonori Kikutake

These are studies of the circular residential units suggested for Marine City. The residential units are fixed onto the central pipe of equipment and structure. The units rotate in order to fulfill the viewing and sunlight demands. Residential units are mass-produced, and the kitchen and the bathroom are in one area. As for furniture, the foot of the bed is designed in a circular shape, the table is wave shaped, and the wardrobe hanger is intensified in an S-shape.

53 Unabaru Marine City, bird's-eye view   *(fig. 47)*

Sketch, 1960
Pencil and ink on tracing paper, 10⅝ x 14¼" (27 x 36 cm.)
Signed: "K. Kikutake 1960 March 10"
Lent by Kiyonori Kikutake

This is the whole view of the Marine City called Unabaru off Tokyo. The city can hold a population of 500 thousand and it is 10 km. in diameter. In the center of the city is a port for submarines; it is surrounded by the residential belt and again

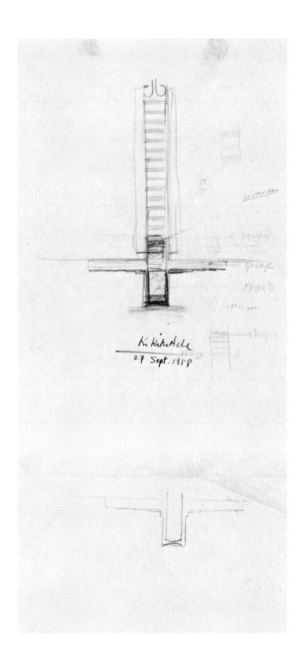

74.   *Kikutake, Tower Shaped City*. No. 48.

Working sketch, 1958
Pencil and red pencil on tracing paper, 13¾ x 6¾" (35 x 17 cm.)
Signed: "K. Kikutake, 27 Sept. 1958"
Lent by Kiyonori Kikutake

by the outer commercial belt and by the outermost break-
water zone. It is a city that floats in the ocean, riding the
currents.

54 Marine City with Nova Block Housing, distant elevation

Working sketch, 1960
Ink on tracing paper, 8⅝ x 6¼" (22 x 16 cm.)
Signed: "K. Kikutake 1960 March 29"
Lent by Kiyonori Kikutake

This sketch shows the floating block of Marine City 1958
with the tower-shaped structure. In the finished form it was
transformed into a sail-like tension structure (cf. no. 51).
"This proposal for marine cities is the first of its kind in the
world. It was the Soviet success in shooting their Sputnik
rocket into space, which led to the publication of this
memorable proposal.
"The civilization of the world may be said to be a continental
civilization, built on land, discovered on land, and having
prospered on land. The continent has been safely supporting
man and promising him happiness and hope, and it appeared
capable of meeting the expectations of mankind. However,
when we look at the history of man, we cannot help but
wonder if man has truly found happiness and hope. The
answer is no. Continental civilization has constantly spread
bloody strife among that mankind fated to live on land. It
may not be too much to say that continental civilization has
been no more than a history of conflict. And today the world
is being daily threatened with the final confrontation
between the two continents. . . .
"The marine city is a proposal to build the world of
tomorrow. Today, mankind is challenging the sea, that sea
which occupies 70% of the earth's surface area, which has
long surveyed continental civilization, and which has
repelled mankind for 5,000 years. It may be said that we are
attempting to face the sea as a unified society.
"The marine city is not simply an attempt to expand the
land. It is also clearly not an idea to escape from the land. As
for escape, the planning is too great, and as for expanding the
land, the concentration of composite technical and economic
power is too great.
"The sea will likely continue to reject unplanned and
disorderly projects. It is reclamation which desecrates this
love of cleanliness of the sea. That the conditions for the

establishment of a superior society cannot be brought about by reclamation is clear from the relations between man and the land. It may be said that technology will lose its meaning unless man's power is concentrated deliberately and coordinately. Techniques for colossal construction cannot bear to be used and must not be allowed to be used for destructive confusion in the name of construction. . . .

"Fresh air, a healthily mild climate, grand natural scenery, a horizon giving a global feeling, the blessings of the sun from sunrise to sunset, the feeling of humanity liberated from race and national boundaries, an orderly social life—the marine city will be born as, and must be made into, a city truly contributing to human society. It must be to create the marine city, not to live in the marine city. . . .

The marine city is not necessarily anchored at any fixed place. It may be shifted to any desirable location necessary. The marine city is a mobile city.

"The construction of the marine city will be started from the construction of a floating manufacturing factory, which might be called its mother ship. From this factory city on the sea will be born one new marine city after another. Self-propagation is also possible. Creating space for the human society, the marine city will create on its underside a reef for fish, which may be used for preserving and breeding fish. The marine city is produced as an artificial city, and, as a manufactured city, may function systematically as a city. These city functions will be offered to a new society of man and hold out great promise for the future of mankind."[57]

Kurokawa, Noriaki (Kisho) (Nagoya, Japan, 1934-   )

Kisho Kurokawa graduated from Kyoto University in 1957 and then studied with Kenzo Tange at the University of Tokyo. He gained prominence in the early 1960s as a member of the Metabolist Group, but his architectural practice did not begin to flourish until the second half of the decade. Among Kurokawa's executed works most closely associated with Metabolism are the plans for two new towns, Hishini (begun 1966) and Fujisawar (begun 1968), and the Nakagin Capsule Tower in Tokyo completed in 1972.

In recent years Kurokawa, without rejecting the convictions informing his previous work, has become identified with Post-Metabolism. His Sony Tower in Osaka (finished 1976) still makes use of clip-on elements, but it has a compositional unity that is often absent in Metabolist structures. Besides heading a large architectural office, Kurokawa chairs a social engineering think tank, serves on a variety of governmental planning commissions, and appears as a commentator on Japanese television.

55   Helix Structure, bird's-eye view   *(fig. 46)*
Freehand rendering, 1960—61
Ink and pen on tracing paper, 10½ x 13⅞" (26.7 x 35.4 cm.)
Unsigned
Lent by Kisho Kurokawa

56   Helix Structure, plan   *(fig. 75)*

Kurokawa designed his Helix Structures for the second Metabolist manifesto (1961). The towers resemble giant DNA molecules, and, just as DNA provides the means by which genetic information is transmitted in life, they form a network that facilitates the transmission of people and things throughout the city. In these studies Kurokawa has emphasized systems rather than individual human beings. He has barely indicated the houses and commercial and public structures that would be attached to or detached from the infra-structures as needed. Instead, he has stressed the flow of traffic hurtling along the roadways or spiraling up in the elevators from the parking garages to the towers. The elevation locates this Meta-polis in what is a rarity in Japan, a flat, open site, but the plan superimposes the Helix Structures on a conventional city and shows how they could be connected to existing transportation systems.

57   "Fiber Form Study," section   *(fig. 57)*
Rendering, 1964/65
Ink on tracing paper, 33¼ x 17¼" (84.5 x 43.8 cm.)
Unsigned
Lent by Kisho Kurokawa

58 "Porous Space Study," plan *(fig. 43)*
Freehand rendering, 1963/64
Pencil on tracing paper over ink on tracing paper, 23⅜ x 16½"
(59.0 x 41.9 cm.)
Unsigned
Lent by Kisho Kurokawa

59 "Meta-Polis," orthographic elevation
Rendering, 1963/64
Pencil on tracing paper over ink on tracing paper, 9¼ x 30" (23.5 x 76.2 cm.)
Lent by Kisho Kurokawa

Kurokawa continued the ideas of urban growth he explored in his Tokyo (1960) and Helix plans in the Metamorphosis Plan conceived for the never-completed Metabolist manifesto of 1965. "Fiber Form Study" and "Porous Space Study" illustrate the two systems of growth in nature that Kurokawa has applied to architectural design. Fiber Form allows expansion along linear patterns in the same way, for example, that branches grow on a tree. Porous Spaces, on the other hand, develop in clusters that can have a linear arrangement as is seen here. Kurokawa has metamorphosized the organic shapes of this drawing into a much more city-like appearance than the forms in the "Fiber Form" drawing, which retains the character of a science text illustration. The root-like lines surrounding the cell clusters suggest the service zones and transportation networks that link the individual "energy points" and "dwelling points" (the Meta-poles) composing Kurokawa's ideal metabolic city.

Though the "Meta-polis" is to be plugged into a system designed according to natural principles, its architectural elements are not based on organic forms. Their silhouettes resemble those found in the science fiction comic books celebrated in the "Zoom" issue of *Archigram* (#4, 1964), published at about the same time as this drawing was made. Whether or not *Archigram* suggested forms that Kurokawa developed in this scheme, the comparison demonstrates the close relationship between English and Japanese architecture in the early 1960s. Kurokawa, however, ordered his fantastic images into a much more plausible scheme than those offered by his British colleagues, and the simple lines of the mountain range behind the Meta-polis complex add a grace note rarely seen in proposals for the high-technology world of the future.

Richard Cleary

75.   *Kurokawa, Helix structure.* No. 56.

Sketch, "April 15, 1961"
Colored pencil on tracing paper, 16¾ x 23⅜" (42.5 x 58.9 cm.)
Signed: "Kuro"
Lent by Kisho Kurokawa

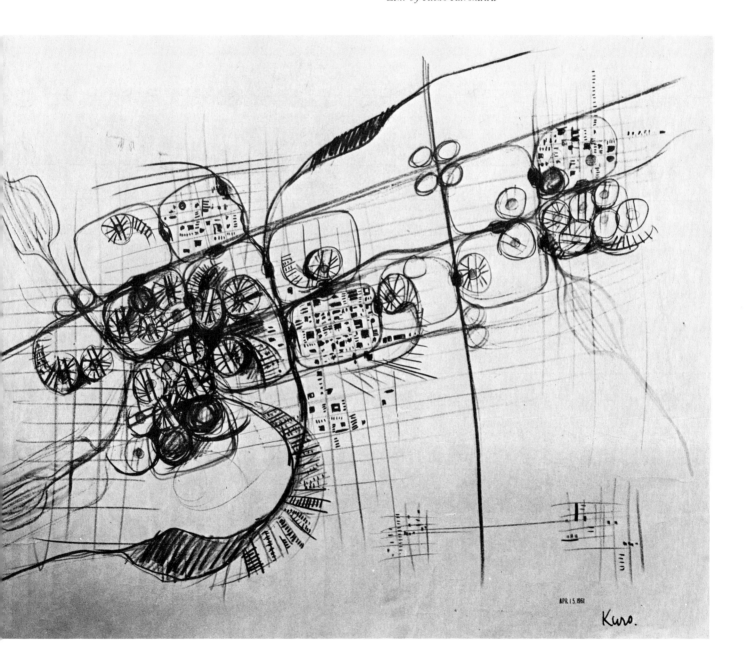

Lamb, Charles R. (New York City, 1860—Cresskill, New Jersey, 1942)

Trained as an artist and architect, Lamb worked as a designer of ecclesiastical interiors in the family stained-glass and mosaic business, of which he was president. A large proportion of his creative energy was spent, however, on his proposals for civic improvements, especially for his home city of New York for which he designed the celebratory Admiral Dewey Arch. His views on architecture and city planning conformed to the most advanced contemporary theories of the City Beautiful movement in the United States, but his proposals for specific remedies for New York's problems of congestion and over-building seem more imaginative and vigorous than most formal City Beautiful plans.
Lamb never considered his schemes "visionary." He continually maintained that "municipal art must have as its foundation practicability"[58] and his plans usually included suggestions on how to finance the proposed improvements.
His city planning ideas appeared regularly in magazines and newspapers from the late 1890s through the first decade of the twentieth century, after which he seems to have grown discouraged by lack of recognition. Many of Lamb's ideas do reappear, without acknowledgement, in the visionary schemes of a number of architects in the 1920s, among the best-known, Hugh Ferriss, Harvey Wiley Corbett (a friend of Lamb's), and Francisco Mujica. It seems likely that these men knew of Lamb's designs.

C.W.

60   "Suggestion for a Model City," overview   *(fig. 2)*
Bird's-eye perspective, c. 1904
Pencil, ink, and watercolor on board, 27¼ x 30½" (69.0 x 77.5 cm.)
Unsigned (signature lost)
Lent by Barea Lamb Seeley, Tenafly, New Jersey and Charles Anthony Lamb, Darien, Connecticut

This project, internationally published at the time,[59] is an early and classic twentieth-century argument for the advantages of planning in hexagons, that is to say, tessellated (i.e., squashed) circular zones of activity incorporating triangular (i.e., diagonal) efficiency of vehicular movement. The idea had been anticipated in the famous Woodward plan for Detroit of c. 1805 and was later to be stressed for regional planning by Walther Christaller and other protagonists of what is called "central place" theory, namely an economics of area rather than time. Lamb wrote about his project:
"After the fullest consideration of all the possibilities that geometric figures give, the writer is tempted to suggest the scheme shown in the accompanying diagram, the hexagon *(fig. 3).* This permits the development of the city to the utmost that might be possible within many decades, because with the hexagon, the great advantage of the diagonal already discussed is secured, and, at the same time, intervening spaces which can be secured for playgrounds and park areas, between the large central areas, which, in turn, can be used for groups of civic buildings in certain parts of the city, and, again, in other parts of the city, seats of learning, recreation, business in all its forms, banking, publishing, the newspaper industries, and the thousand and one trades, which, in their turn, seem to be desirous of grouping themselves around a common center . . . . The power of extension of such a plan is infinite. The danger of congestion by the excessive growth of cities has in such a plan been eliminated, or, at least, reduced to its minimum."[60]
G.R.C.

61   Streets High in the Air, elevation, "How the proposed terraced building will compare with the present tower form."   *(fig. 76)*

62   Streets High in the Air, elevation   *(fig. 10)*

Rendering, c. 1908
Watercolor and pastel on grey paper, 33 x 23½" (83.8 x 59.7 cm.)
Unsigned
Lent by Barea Lamb Seeley, Tenafly, New Jersey and Charles Anthony Lamb, Darien, Connecticut

Rendering, 1908
Pen and ink on board, 32¾ x 24¼" (83.2 x 61.6 cm.)
Signed: "Vernon Howe Bailey," the delineator
Lent by Barea Lamb Seeley, Tenafly, New Jersey and Charles Anthony
Lamb, Darien, Connecticut

Lamb is one of the forgotten fathers of the visionary tradition of the skyscraper city. In 1908, the year of their execution, these two drawings of Lamb's proposal for streets in the air and a stepped-back form for skyscrapers represent very early examples of concepts that were to become popular aspects of the futuristic urban imagery of the 1920s: however, these drawings actually illustrate ideas that Lamb had first presented ten years earlier (1898) in an article in *Municipal Affairs*, the magazine of the Reform Club of New York, entitled, "Civic Architecture from its Constructive Side."

Although Lamb was himself an artist, he often employed his friend, the illustrator Vernon Howe Bailey (1874-1953), to visualize his proposals. Bailey was a popular delineator of city scenes, known for his fresh, rough-sketch style; he collaborated with authors on a number of books, published in magazines, and served on the art staff of several newspapers. The pen and ink drawing of Lamb's idea for elevated pedestrian streets and stepped-back skyscrapers was commissioned for an article in the magazine section of the *New York Herald* of August 9, 1908, entitled "Saving the Sunshine in the City's Valley of Shadow." The need to find a way to preserve some light and air on the New York streets, a problem since the boom in tall building construction in the 1890s, was a fervent public issue in 1908, due to the recent completion of the Singer Building and the predictions of one-thousand-foot towers. Many suggestions for building code revisions or zoning restrictions were advanced, and Lamb revived his 1898 proposals, calling for legislation to restrict the maximum height of a building's facade over the street to 125 feet. After this height, the building would be stepped back in stages according to an angle determined by the width of the street (modification of a French law); at the center of the site, the tower could rise to almost unlimited height. At the level of the first set-back, a pedestrian street would connect buidings between blocks and provide a new, attractive shopping area. Bailey's drawing illustrates Lamb's proposal on the left side of the picture and contrasts its order with the chaos, on the right, that would reign if building were to continue without far-sighted planning.

The second, pastel illustration of bridges connecting skyscrapers (no. 62) is by Lamb's own hand and was probably prepared for the 1908 exhibition organized by the Commission on the Congestion of Population, of which Lamb was a member.

Carol Willis

Le Corbusier (Charles Edouard Jeanneret Gris) (La Chaux-de-Fonds, Switzerland, 1887 — Roquebrune, Cap-Martin, France, 1965)

In the spring of 1961 Le Corbusier visited Columbia University in New York City to lecture and to be celebrated. He was described as follows in the official university news release:
"Designer of distinguished buildings, including the Ministry of Education and Public Health in Rio de Janeiro, the new Museum of Modern French Art in Tokyo, and the Palace of Centrosoyus in Moscow, Le Corbusier contributed fundamentally to the plans for the United Nations Secretariat building. He has also designed Harvard's Visual Arts Center, his first building in the United States. Le Corbusier holds no architectural degrees, and practices architecture in France under a special decree from the French government. He has, however, received numerous honors including the American Institute of Architects gold medal for 1961."
He was presented with an honorary degree by Columbia's president, Grayson Kirk, who read the following citation in an impressive ceremony in the rotunda of the university's Low Memorial Library:
"Charles Edouard Le Corbusier, eminent theoretician, profound architectural innovator, inventor of the skyscraper-studded park, you have resolutely proclaimed Man's right to an environment of increased amenities.
Through your architecture, you have sought to bring Man and the Forces of Nature into beneficent accord. In a technical age you have endeavored to produce a Universal Man, a concept designed to give unity and validity to creative achievement in those broad fields of the Arts upon which your abundant energies have been so productively expended.
"In recognition of both your sustained ideals and your positive accomplishments, by the powers vested in me by the Trustees of Columbia University, I bestow on you the degree of Doctor of Humane Letters, honoris causa."

63   Drawings for a lecture on The Necessity for Communal Plans: A New Day of the Machinist Civilization

Three sets of inter-related sketches and diagrams, 19 November, 1935, at Columbia University, Low Memorial Library
Pastel on paper, 42¼ x 20'4⅞"   (108 cm. x 6.22 m.)
Unsigned, undated
Lent by the Avery Architectural Library, Columbia University

When in the winter of 1935-36 Le Corbusier travelled in the United States—a visit that both provoked, and was described in, his *Quand les cathédrales étaient blanches (When the Cathedrals Were White)* of 1937—he lectured at a number of places, including Columbia University where he made this long sheet of drawings as he talked. In Chicago he titled his talk "The Great Waste," and this drawing is a literal illustration of that lecture as printed on pp. 171-78, 186-89 of his book.
Retrospectively he described his message as follows: "In my lectures in the U.S.A., I tried to make it clear that that was the fatal American waste, paid for by a new and unconscious slavery. The hours lost in getting to innumerable suburban communities are nothing *by comparison with the daily hours lost by everyone, over and above truly productive work,* in order to pay for that mistake! For the gigantic suburbs, house after house, swallow up an incredibly tangled network of railroads, highways, service lines for water, gas, electricity, telephone. I ask you: who pays for that? We do, you do, everyone does every day, through the tribute of three or four hours of sterile work given in order to pay for these futilities, given by every one of you in order to make wind, in order to find an occasional tree, a little patch of sky, along roads made dangerous by cars. When you can have many trees, a great deal of sky, a vast amount of space and no cars to contend with, if you agree to return to the city, to Manhattan, on condition that you made Manhattan—a vast and quite sufficient area—a "radiant city," that is, a city dedicated to the necessary and satisfying human joys."[61]

64   Drawings for an address on linear decentralization   *(fig. 58)*

Inter-related sketches and diagrams, 28 April 1961, Columbia University, Low Memorial Library
Pastel on paper, 42½ x 71½"   (107.3 x 181.6 cm.)
Unsigned and undated
Lent by the Avery Architectural Library, Columbia University

Le Corbusier drew as he talked: "This is the agricultural milieu with the ox, the horse, the much larger tractor, and the cooperative center.

"Here at the crossroads of two roads, I am drawing the beginning of a radioconcentric center, the grocery store, the inn, the hardware store, which go back as far as antiquity, even before the invention of nails; the center which has come to be the source of all exchange. This is the radiocenter of exchange.

"The logical consequence of this was the multiplication of this phenomenon, the creation of a city with tentacles, the sprawling city, which developed in a dramatic manner—I am writing 'sprawling city.' These must disappear, these must die, must fall back into proportion and find the size best suited for proper exchange.

"Now we are witnessing the birth of the linear city of changes, the linear industrial city which moves in around the waterways, the roadways, and the railways, all of which bring in raw materials and which take away the manufactured goods. Along the whole length of this linear industrial city, there shall be dwelling places, building proportionate in size. These meet at the two radioconcentric cities at the extremities, with a distance between them of one or two hundred kilometers....

"I shall finish this sketch with a picture I shall draw here: the monument of the open hand, which is my only political intervention in fifty years; the open hand, open to receive and to give. With this gesture, which has no negative political quality, but only a positive human meaning, you open the doors to human sentiments of generosity, just as this evening you have risked opening the doors of academism to me."[62]

65   Drawings for an address on engineers, architects . . . and the cosmos   *(fig. 77)*

"I shall end my slight intervention with geography. (I use the color orange in order to avoid the red—because it is useless to try to make colors say the contrary of what one means). Here I am drawing a country—I said I was becoming a geographer; here I shall place the linear industrial city, which aligns the three roads, land, water, and rail, going through the tunnels and linking them together.

"You will find and follow those roads even if they lead far away—what does it matter? Far away there are men like us; these roads follow the old roads of History, all the way to China. And at the end of these roads, I will take another

color, blue, to show the context and continuity, and here I shall draw the building of Columbia University. I'm less good at drawing the United States—I may make mistakes, but anyway, here are the lines of continuity and the sense of continuity which tie things together.

"I shall finish this talk and my sketch by this: two hands, one opposite the other; one is red, and no political aspersion is intended, and the other blue. They represent a friendly dialogue, a brotherly dialogue from beginning to end: and I sign, "Columbia, 28/4/61, a grateful Le Corbusier."[63]

66   Drawings for a lecture on architects in regional planning   *(fig. 17)*

Inter-related sketches and diagrams, 28 April 1961, Columbia University, in architectural studio
Pastel on paper, 42¼ x 71⅝" (107.3 x 181.9 cm.)
Signed: "L-C 28/4/61"
Lent by the Avery Architectural Library, Columbia University

"I draw a road—and another road; here at the intersection is the beginning of a radioconcentric group. The phenomenon develops and multiplies into wider and wider belts, and an unquestionable radioconcentric network is established.

"I write: radioconcentric city of exchanges: goods, ideas, and government, because there is another human establishment that exists; its name is the unit of agricultural exploitation, which is the first event of land occupancy by men. The third human establishment, the linear city of the industrial age, does not exist yet, and if it were created, it would soon bring the world conjunctural solutions, among them the casting away of tentacular (from tentacle) radioconcentric cities, and would bring about unity, union, and fraternity among countries by creating contacts by economic units of favorable sizes.

"The evolution of this city in a machinist civilization must be geographical first. This is a radioconcentric unit that has been started, has evolved thus, and constitutes an unquestionable element of radioconcentric nature, absolutely the opposite of the parallel system of the linear city. Paris is an example of a city that has spread into suburbs, thus introducing the problem of distance. This city has become an absolute drama, similar to the drama that weighs upon New York, Berlin, Moscow, London: the drama of the tentacular city. Facing this dramatic situation means going somewhere

77. *Le Corbusier, Lecture drawings.* No. 65.

Inter-related sketches and diagrams, 28 April 1961, Columbia
University, Low Memorial Library
Pastel on paper, 42¼ x 71½"   (107.3 x 181.6 cm.)
Signed: "Columbia 28/4/61 L.-C."
Lent by the Avery Architectural Library, Columbia University

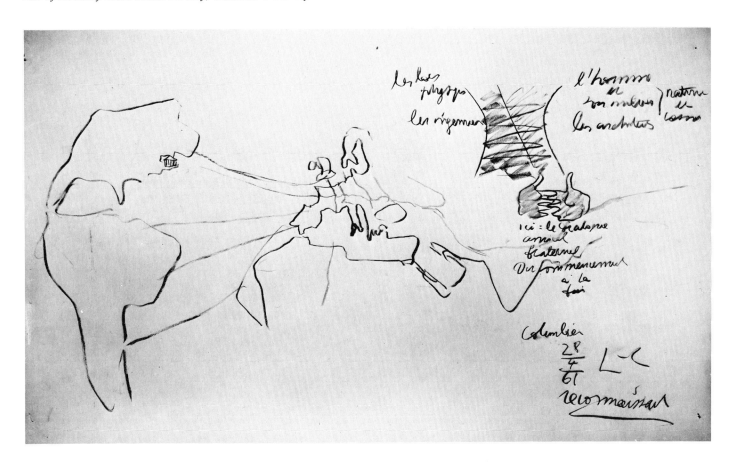

into enormous spaces. These main roads will have to be created, or those, synthesized by this essential diagram: here you have the road to Spain, to Italy, Germany, to the North, to the West."[64]

As the French words on these drawings of Le Corbusier are so intricately locked into their sketches and diagrams, we have not tried to list them all in the catalogue. Instead we advise the visitor to read for exhibition nos. 64 and 65, pp. 164-167 of *The Great Makers of Modern Architecture* (see note 62), for no. 66, pp. 168-171 of the same publication, and for no. 63, pp. 171-178, 186-191 of *When the Cathedrals Were White* (see note 61).

Le Ricolais, G. Robert (La Roche-sur-Yon, France, 1894—Paris, 1977)

Engineer, poet, and painter, Le Recolais was innovative in each of his callings. Awarded in 1935 the Medal of the Society of Civil Engineers of France for his research on "lightweight metal structures"; in 1962, the Grand Prix du Cercle d'Etudes Architecturales of France for his "research and its contribution to architecture"; in 1976, the American Institute of Architects medal for contributions to the profession.
His work includes: structures for French railways, 1947, the Ministry of Finance, 1948, and other buildings from 1954 to 1959; paintings on permanent exhibition at the Musée de Nantes; poems published by Cahiers de l'Ecole de Rochefort; over fifty major published writings and over sixty major unpublished writings.
He was Professor of Architecture at the University of Pennsylvania from 1953 to 1977.

67   Starhex network, bird's-eye view, plans, and diagrams   *(fig. 4)*

Sketches, 1962-68
Red and black ballpoint pen on paper (drawing also on verso), 11 x 8½" (28 x 21.5 cm.)
Unsigned
Lent by the School of Architecture, University of Pennsylvania

68   Fishbridge in the starhex network, perspective *(fig. 78)*

69   "Fishbridge" or double parabolic trihex bridge for Skyrail, elevation and sections

Sketches, 1962-68
Red ballpoint pen on lined paper, 11 x 8½" (28 x 21.5 cm.)
Unsigned
Lent by the School of Architecture, University of Pennsylvania

70   Starhex network (plan), and double parabolic tension net bridge for the Skyrail (elevation)

Sketches, 1962-68
Red, blue, and black ballpoint pen and pencil on verso of mimeographed newsletter,   11 x 8½" (28 x 21.5 cm.)
Unsigned
Lent by the School of Architecture, University of Pennsylvania

Triaxial Networks for Urban Circulation and Skyrail Structures for Aerial Mass-Transit (1962-68)[65]
"To research what? Research of what? . . . zero weight, infinite span . . . You know it can't be done, but at least it's a limit that we could try to go to. It's a desire, a human desire to do . . . man never satisfied with himself—he wants to transcend himself, or to find some kind of thing that doesn't exist. He wants to go farther. Of course it's a way of devastating yourself, because there is just no end to it.
"It is somehow surprising how much is known about the flow of gases, fluids, and electrons and how little about the circulation of human beings . . . with railway systems you can handle 60,000 passengers per hour on a single line, which is equivalent to the maximum performance of a 20-lane highway . . . this terrifying problem of number.
"Maybe, too, our notion of static, crystallized form is often an

illusion given by our defective senses. We no longer have the plaza of ancient Rome for our forum, but some kind of nervous system enabling people to come in contact with others and get to their business in the shortest and fastest way . . . Our future objective may not be at all how to structure buildings, but how to structure circulations.

"We need more efficient systems for this intercommunication of urban space, and a prerequisite will be some better arrangement of potential routes, with a minimum number of intersections. The Starhex network (no. 67) would be a quite good theoretical pattern to consider: compared with an orthogonal grid over an equivalent area, the length of streets between intersections being equal, some simple calculation shows that the Starhex network has at least 13.5 percent fewer intersections, that the combined length of streets would be shorter by at least 13.5 percent, and that the average route would be about 12 percent shorter. (A network of all hexagons or all triangles may be even more efficient in some ways, but you would lose either straight line movement or reasonably simple intersections).[66] The triaxial distribution of the Starhex network also gives a much richer combinatorial potentiality than orthogonal distribution. In fact it corresponds to the introduction of a new alphabet—not only producing new sounds but also allowing a given message to be conveyed in a much shorter time; this reflects a law of cybernetics, that the length of a message is inversely proportional to the logarithm of the number of signs in the code being used, resulting in the apparent paradox that the more ways there are, the less we have to use them.

" . . . think of the Paris Metro, without which life in that city would be impossible . . . Unfortunately, building a transit system in the bowels of the earth today, you would have insurmountable problems getting around the endless networks of pipes and wires and foundations. The ground surface also is totally occupied by buildings and streets. So the alternative we have considered is an aerial system of mass transit, superimposed on the city.

"The Skyrail system (no. 68) we have proposed would consist of a Starhex network of aerial bridges spanning about 1,600 feet between interchange stations. These stations would be incorporated into buildings 30 to 40 stories high, and each one would connect two lines with banks of elevators and escalators leading to 300-foot platforms, where trains would arrive every 90 seconds.

It seems also that there would be some extremely exciting

value in superimposing on the rather confused tissue of an existing metropolis an order directed toward integration, to counter the kind of dislocation created by highways . . . With a system of elevated transit, we could perhaps open up a new, or lost dimension—the aerial view of the city, the city being seen as a whole without losing the feeling of orientation.

"*Trihex bridge for the Skyrail* (nos. 69, 70) . . . a Skyrail system based on a continuity of tension between spans has the drawback of being restricted to absolutely straight lines. It may be more convenient to locate stations on a more flexible path. So we went back to a less efficient structure in terms of weight, but a system easier to construct and of a more classical character; the bridge becomes a self-contained body, with no structural connection between adjacent spans required . . . with a span of 1,600 feet the distance between apices would be about 80 feet. Under maximum loading—two convoys of 250 tons each at midspan—the cable elongation would be about 16 inches, yielding a deflection of 20 feet . . . . The controlled deflection could even provide trains with a certain amount of acceleration on leaving one station and deceleration on entering the next; a sag of 20 feet would give a rolling train a velocity of 25 miles per hour at midspan, and this convenience should result in an economical power system, both in terms of weight and kilowatts.

If you want to build in space, your mind cannot remain in the plane."

Peter McCleary

78.   *Le Ricolais, Fishbridge in the Starhex network.* No. 68.

Sketch, 1962-68
Red ballpoint pen on paper, 8½ x 11" (21.5 x 28 cm.)
Unsigned
Lent by the School of Architecture, University of Pennsylvania

Malcolmson, Reginald (Dublin, Ireland 1912-)

Malcolmson is a visionary architect and a proponent of the linear city. His architectural projects were first exhibited in Ireland in 1943-44 and later in the 50s and 60s were published and shown in Chicago, New York, Los Angeles, London, Paris, Tokyo, Lima, Santiago, and Buenos Aires. His work is the subject of a travelling exhibition entitled "Visionary Projects" in which the major themes are linear cities, suspended buildings, extensible buildings, industrialized houses, and color in building.
He was educated and practiced as an architect in Ireland before coming to the United States in 1947 to study with Mies van der Rohe at Illinois Institute of Technology, Chicago. Subsequently he joined the faculty at IIT (1949-64), was assistant to the director (1953-58) and acting director (1958-59).
In Chicago he worked with Konrad Wachsmann on the design of prefabricated buildings and with Ludwig Hilberseimer on city-planning projects including industrial studies for Chicago and housing in Detroit.
He was dean of the College of Architecture and Design at the University of Michigan from 1964-74, where he is currently teaching.

71   Theater, interior elevation   *(fig. 79)*

The theater is contained in a long-span structure of glass and steel. Clear and simple elements related spatially create an environment which focuses all attention on the actors and the drama: the stage is a simple elevated platform with a scene wall; the seating area is on a steel frame structure with a suspended mezzanine; an acoustical shell of stainless steel hangs above the stage. These architectural elements are in color so that the magic atmosphere of the theater is intensified.
Actors and audience alike are elevated above the ground— confronting each other in space at a level to which they must ascend—a solemn and symbolic act.

72   Metrolinear I, view   *(fig. 25)*

Perspective rendering, June 1955
Ink on illustration board, 40 x 30"   (101.5 x 76 cm.)
Unsigned
Lent by Reginald Malcolmson

Metrolinear I was first exhibited as part of a faculty exhibition at IIT at the time of the dedication of Crown Hall on the campus in Chicago.
This drawing belongs to the first series of linear city studies—in this case, of the metropolitan center developed on linear principles. The great auto route runs between the parking strip and office towers. Bridges cross the route. The office towers stand in open parkland.

73   Museum of Natural Sciences, interior elevation

Perspective, 1957
Ink with photo and collage elements on illustration board, 30 x 40"   (76 x 101.5 cm.)
Signed on back
Lent by Reginald Malcolmson

The museum is one of a series of large hall structures projected in the 50s and 60s in the investigation of the spatial qualities and architectural possibilities of such enormous interiors. In this project the structure is externalized.
Scientific objects—mesozoic reptiles, meteorites, photo-murals of galaxies, armillary spheres, etc., can be freely

79.   *Malcolmson, Theater.* No. 71.

Orthographic projection, 1949
Collage in color of silk-screen paper, charcoal papers, metal foil,
and India ink on illustration board, 30 x 40"   (76 x 101.5 cm.)
Signed on back
Lent by Reginald Malcolmson

related in the enclosed space.

A large-scale replica of the moon suspended in space contains a planetarium in its interior, which can be reached from a mezzanine level.

The museum presents a great plastic event in an architectural space of limitless possibilities—union of art and science.

74   Metrolinear II, panorama   *(fig. 26)*

Bird's-eye sketch for construction of a scale model, 1960
Black wax pencil on onion skin paper, 36 x 72" (91.5 x 183 cm.)
Unsigned
Lent by Reginald Malcolmson

The panorama shows a central spinal axis of transportation routes on several levels with civic, cultural, and commercial activities on the roof decks reserved solely for pedestrians. Along the margins are office towers, large complexes for sports, festivals, museums, etc., and residential zones. Further from the main axis are parallel farm belts, while beyond these are the routes serving large-scale industries whose separation from the city guarantees clean air. This is the linear metropolis, flexible in its structure and theoretically capable of continuous expansion.

Drawing is often thought of as simply a means to an end,
—to convey information by graphic methods
—a form of communication.

Not so.
While at the most simplistic and primitive level,
this may seem to be true,
Drawing is much more
—for it has an inner meaning.

Drawing is the mastery of reality
in which, by very simple, but essentially subtle means,
in the formation of planes and volumes,
linear structures evolve.

So that, the creative architect
is one who captures these pure products
of the constructive imagination,
these three-dimensional space concepts,
and turns them as though by magic into a series of signs and
     symbols
calculated to convey to the knowing and sensitive observer
the idea of something, which can only at that moment,
exist in a future, yet to be realized.

So a drawing may become a thing in itself
it may reveal the poetic and the sublime
in visionary form
that must await the day of its realization
with the knowledge that the day may never come.

Drawing is to Architecture
as the first and often the purest evidence
of the creative spirit,
revealing even if only as a simple diagram
the idea awaiting its translation into material form.

Reginald Malcolmson

Mendelsohn, Eric [Erich] (Allenstein, Germany, 1887—San Francisco, 1953)

Eric Mendelsohn, who built many buildings in Europe, the Near East, and America, was the prototypical visionary architect. Graduate of the Technischen Hochschulen of Berlin and Munich (1914), he received intense stimulation for architecture in his World War I experiences. He visited and published about the United States in 1924, and immigrated in 1941, having left Germany in 1933 for England and Palestine.
As he himself commented (UCLA 1948): "In 1917, with the Kaiser's Army at the Russian front, in the unreal world of dug-outs and trenches, my architectural dreams are the only reality. But, the physical and mental compression of danger and destruction ever-present condense the extensive scale to somewhat smaller and more compact projects . . . . What then, in 1917, is an unconscious emanation of my artistic nature, reveals, I am now aware, nothing else but the architectural method of counterpoint, entirely alike the counterpoint in music, where one or several melodies are added as accompaniment to a given melody. . . . It also explains the frequent references on my sketches to Bach, Stravinsky, or other composers. A fact which does not mean that I am prone to confound the strict limits of our art with other artistic media."[67]
And in a letter of 1917 to his friend Erwin F. Freundlich, the astrophysicist, "My sketches are data, the contour lines of an instantaneous vision. In accordance with their architectural nature, their immediate appearance is that of a whole, and this is how they must be taken.[68]

75   Untitled drawings, elevations (bottom one possibly based on Einstein Tower, Potsdam)   *(fig. 20)*

Sketches, January 1953
Pastel on tracing paper, 21 x 25⅜"   (53.3 x 64.0 cm.)
Signed: "Eric Mendelsohn. I write as I speak. I sketch as I write."
Lent by the University of Oregon Library, Architecture and Allied Arts Branch, Eugene, Oregon   (No. 6)

76   Untitled drawing, elevation   *(fig. 53)*

Sketch, January 1953
Pastel on tracing paper, 21 x 23⅜"   (53.3 x 58.9 cm.)
Unsigned
Lent by the University of Oregon Library, Architecture and Allied Arts Branch, Eugene, Oregon   (No. 14)

77 Untitled drawings, elevations (superimposed)   *(fig. 80)*

These drawings, among others, were made as Mendelsohn lectured to students at the University of Oregon in late January 1953 *(fig. 21)*. As it is difficult to know what he intended to emphasize to them with the sketches—because his lecture was not recorded—it might be enlightening to quote from two of his writings:
"Creative acts—the child's first sensations of body or mind, the engineer's inventions, the artist's conceptions, the revelations of the mystic—are based on visions, on the intuitive recognition of positive facts and potential consequences. This sudden appearance, as in a dream or trance, of existence or of a yet unexperienced workability, a shape or truth not known before, is characterized by an intense concentration on material objects or mental phenomena. To the architect who thrives on his creative and inventive faculty, visions are the vitamins necessary to his artistic functions. Though the nature of the problems with which he is occupied and which he attempts to solve are mostly practical, the organization of space, its structural support and final appearance demand the constant presence of knowledge and research, incessant control, the will-power to coordinate facts and figures, means and desires. . . .
"I remember, when, following my first lecture in the United States (at Columbia University's Architectural School), the students asked me whether I could redraw for them the first visionary sketch of one of my early buildings. I did not

question the reasons for their request, though I know from my own college years how prone to suspicion and inquiry students are. Closing my eyes for a moment in order to recall—after two decades—site, plan and appearance, the 6B in my hand drew in one stroke the significant outline of that specific building. As a matter of fact, I recollected only the unforgettable moment when after much work and many trials the finished design seemed to equal my vision, became final and intelligible.

"Architectural visions, however, are not confined to actual projects. Photographs and descriptions of new experiments in building often stir the artistic imagination to imaginary sketches. Having no real existence, they are mere notes of space and time, three-dimensional and rhythmic expressions of our age's material and mental propensities.

"Many architects must certainly feel this urge, and have had this experience, but only a few seem to be willing to forget their common sense: to take their architectural dreams not as an artistic trick or pictorial magic, and to put them on paper as potential motives for future work. Or, as one of my college professors said, many have visions but only a few are able to depict them.[69]

As regards the act of drawing, he wrote to his wife in 1917:

"The representation has nothing to do with nature, for it takes its laws from architecture itself. Dynamic masses are to be shown so that their dynamism is clearly expressed, so that movement and counter-movement show the balance. Between the two coefficients of direction—energies and sounds—stands the sudden transition, from light to shade, from black to white. Their pauses are the pivots of the movement. They are the impulse, the living element, while the mass is stable. According to the way it is built up, this mass can be mighty, oppressive or finely and sensitively outlined, without losing its stability. The pause stands at the point where the movement is to be given a new and unexpected direction. That is why it surprises, why it stimulates. . . .

"I live among incessant visions. Their transcendence is such that it often carries me away. It is hard to catch it and impossible to grasp it fully: to express it in solid terms is the task. But I am glad to be subject to its law, because for me it is the truest life. . . ."[70]

80.   *Mendelsohn, Untitled Drawing (cropped on right).* No. 77

Sketches, January 1953
Pastel on tracing paper, 18⅝ x 23¼"   (47.3 x 59.1 cm.)
Unsigned
Lent by the University of Oregon Library, Architecture and Allied
Arts Branch, Eugene, Oregon   (No. 10)

Mies van der Rohe, Ludwig (Aachen, Germany, 1886—Chicago, 1969)

Mies van der Rohe, a purist in architectural design, learned the building craft as a stonecutter's apprentice, as office draughtsman, and as assistant in a number of architectural offices, so it is surprising that he should have produced, in the interval of German Expressionist architecture following World War I, several totally abstract, theoretical designs—i.e., paper projects—that were profoundly to affect the course of modernism for several decades. His built style of minimal forms, of rich materials, and flowing space that gives the misleading impression of being reductionist, moved quickly away from the Expressionist mode, and when he came to the United States in 1937 his beautifully proportioned, elegantly framed and glazed houses and his starkly vitreous high-rise towers became the American idea of "modern" for a generation. The prominent role that he had played in the Deutscher Werkbund in the 1920s, in the Bauhaus in the 1930s, and as Director of Architecture for the Illinois Institute of Technology in this country argued for the fact that his formalist principles were not idle abstractions. The drawing that we exhibit is for the project that was, perhaps, most prophetic of what the urban skyline would look like in the late 20th century.

78 "GLAS-HOCH-HAUS," elevation *(fig. 81)*

Mies himself described the intention of this project in the last of four "seasonal" issues of *Frühlicht*, a magazine that Bruno Taut published in Magdeburg during 1921-22 and called "a series on the realization of modern building ideas:"
"Skyscrapers reveal their bold structural pattern during construction. Only then does the gigantic steel web seem impressive. When the outer walls are put in place, the structural system which is the basis of all artistic design is hidden by a chaos of meaningless and trivial forms. When finished, these buildings are impressive only because of their size; yet they could surely be more than mere examples of our technical ability. Instead of trying to solve the new problems with old forms, we should develop the new forms from the very nature of the new problems.
"We can see the new structural principles most clearly when we use glass in place of the outer walls, which is feasible today since in a skeleton building these outer walls do not actually carry weight. The use of glass imposes new solutions. . . . .
"At first glance the curved outline of the plan seems arbitrary. These curves, however, were determined by three factors: sufficient illumination of the interior, the massing of the building viewed from the street, and lastly the play of reflections. I proved in the glass model that calculations of light and shadow do not help in designing an all-glass building."[71]

81.   *Mies van der Rohe, Glass Skyscraper.* No. 78.

Rendering, 1921-22
Charcoal, brown chalk, conté crayon on brown paper mounted on
board, 54½ x 32¾" (138.5 x 83.2 cm.)
Scale: "1:100"
"Mies van der Rohe"
Lent by the Mies van der Rohe Archive, Museum of Modern Art,
New York City

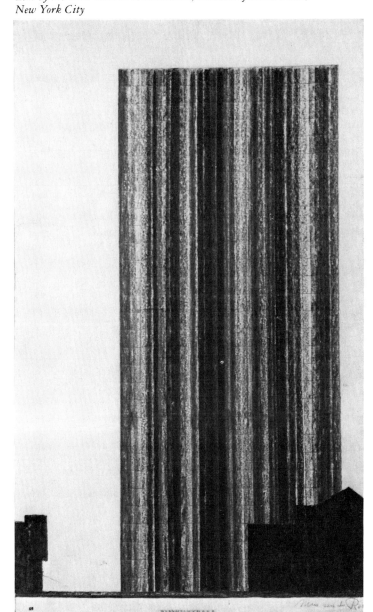

Neutra, Richard (Vienna, 1892—Wuppertal, Germany, 1970)

Neutra's importance as a catalyst between European and American developments in architecture and planning of the 1920s/1930s cannot be overemphasized. Trained in the waning years of Vienna's cultural ferment, Neutra was to participate in the exciting Berlin commissions of Erich Mendelsohn's office before coming to the United States in 1923. Here he conferred with Louis Sullivan in his last days and worked a season with Frank Lloyd Wright. He set up an office in Los Angeles that soon included such important young American architects as Harwell Harris and Gregory Ain, who worked briefly on the Rush City project. He designed a number of classic West Coast houses, but also pursued the dream of a new American city arrangement that would combine the speed and efficiency of American technology with the social amiability of Old World street life—a project that he called "Rush City Reformed."

In these same years—the late 1920s, early 1930s—he also reported back to Central Europe in book form on the advances in modern building techniques in America. He became an important member of the C.I.A.M. (Congrès Internationaux d'Architecture Moderne) and exchanged interesting correspondence on such matters with his English counterpart, Maxwell Fry, an individual with whom he had much in common, although Fry felt that Rush City was too robot-like for British taste.

As regards the drawings, it would seem that Rush City was the model on which Neutra worked out and tested his designs for interrelated structures and people—i.e., urbanism. The reason that the Rush City project is dated differently by the various Neutra biographers is that it was one of the several longtime preoccupations with which he was beset as an urbanistic architect. All of its drawings, including those that we exhibit, are undated or can only be dated by their first published appearance.[72] There are some basic changes in the same views of the project as published in Shelter *magazine in 1938 and in the retrospective catalogue edited by Boesiger of 1951. For instance, there is a transformation in the layout of residential areas (not shown in drawings on exhibit) wherein he later incorporates budding cul-de-sac Neighborhood-Plan residential streets that he had used in his Park Living Colony of 1939 in Jacksonville, Florida—very likely under C.I.A.M. influence.*

His Rush City plan is organized with respect to the speed and efficiency of circulation of vehicles and people, achieved by the laying out of linear axes and the segregation by speed and purpose of traffic—including pedestrians—by bridges, streets of various levels, and sunken viaducts. He said, "Thinned habitation density, a consequence of motor car use, calls for increased traffic area in the central district and in a number of auxiliary decentralized business districts. Production plants, as employment markets, should be so located that irrational commuting of employees is minimized...."[73]

79   Rush City Reformed, overview of radial avenue (1-2) and perpendicular boulevard connection (3-3-2)   *(fig. 15)*

Perspective rendering, 1923
Graphite on tracing paper, 12½ x 16½" (31.8 x 42 cm.)
Unsigned
Lent by U.C.L.A., University Research Library

Boulevard runs left to right between the business "distributional" zone with its connecting bridges and the smaller transit apartments. In the foreground are residential blocks and greenbelt with Radial Plan school. Major linear axis (never detailed in his drawings) runs left to right above the drawing.

80   Rush City Reformed, bird's-eye view of downtown city "distributional" blocks   *(fig. 82)*

City blocks are narrow, without courts, for more sunlight at street level. Ground level is composed entirely of mechanized traffic, with railroads sunken. Shopping areas and pedestrians are elevated, with continuously running elevators at street intersections. The analogy to Russian Constructivist design is obvious.

81   Rush City Reformed, bird's-eye view of terminal

Perspective rendering, 1923-27
Graphite on linen, 13½ x 17½" (34.3 x 44.5 cm.)
Unsigned
Lent by U.C.L.A., University Research Library

This terminal for through traffic presumably sits at one end of the linear axis, making Rush City only a partially, not an infinitely, linear model. Long-distance trains arrive at lowest level with city rapid-transit and waiting rooms above. The relation to New York's Grand Central Terminal and to Sant'Elia is clear in the segregated levels, but Sant'Elia's was a central (union) station, whereas this "terminal" seems to be placed at the end of a metrolinear axis at that point at which the "suburbs" (whatever they may be called) of a linear city begin.

82. *Neutra, Rush City Reformed.* No. 80.

Perspective rendering, 1923-27
Graphite on linen, 9 x 10″ (23 x 25.4 cm.)
Unsigned
Lent by U.C.L.A., University Research Library

Otto, Frei (Siegmar, Germany, 1925-)

As a youth, Frei Otto was drawn to lightweight structures in the form of gliders which he designed and flew. He was a pilot briefly during the Second World War, and began his study of architecture afterwards. Otto received his doctorate from the Berlin Institute of Technology in 1954. Starting in 1955, Frei Otto developed an impressive series of tensile structures, beginning with small bandstand enclosures and culminating in the German Pavilion at Montreal (1967). In 1964 he founded the Institute for Light Surface Structures at the Technological University at Stuttgart, where, except for extensive travels and outside teaching, he has remained ever since. Frei Otto has collaborated with architects on many of his projects, including Rolf Gutbrod for the Montreal Pavilion and a conference center in Riyadh, Saudi Arabia, and Kenzo Tange for a competition for the Kuwait Sports Center in 1968. In 1972 Otto designed the enclosures for the stadia at the XX Olympics in Munich. Frei Otto has long seen the possibilities for very large tensile structures to shelter whole cities from hostile environments. From 1953 on he has produced a series of visionary, large-scale projects for cities in the Arctic and Antarctica as well as outer space.

82   City Partly Covered by Hung Roof, bird's-eye view *(fig. 35)*

Perspective sketch, 1963
Pencil on light board, sprayed with fixative, 11 ¾ x 15 ¾" (29.8 x 40.0 cm.)
Signed: "Frei Otto 63"
Lent by Frei Otto

A very large tent structure is hung from a central supporting compression arch. The project was eventually exhibited as a scheme at Expo '67 in Montreal, as it is intended for a cold northern climate. Frei Otto wrote of it: "For a major city in a cool region an inter-urban park is to be laid out as a recreational, sports and entertainment center which can continue to function all year round. In the cold season a large portion of the city area, about three square kilometers in size, is covered with a transparent envelope which is so designed that it closes whenever the temperature falls below ten degrees centigrade and opens out again when the temperature rises above this value."[74]
A full range of recreational facilities are provided. There are a number of theaters and sports arenas, both open and enclosed. There are busy precincts, markets, and shopping streets as well as quiet areas with museums. Typically, Otto sees this project in real terms: "At the present time [1964], the cost of constructing a giant envelope... involves an outlay of about 300 million DM. This is not a considerable expense in relation to the possibility of intensive utilization by thousands of people every day and by millions in the course of each year."[75]

83   Main Pedestrian Artery in a Large Densely Populated City   *(fig. 83)*

This is a sketch of a main pedestrian thoroughfare or "concentration point" in one of Frei Otto's cities of the future. A canal, complete with gondolas, functions as a primary circulation artery; circulation is further distributed by a network of individual cars suspended from rails and by an undulating series of overlapping pedestrian ramps and terraces. The cars seat from three to five persons and are guided automatically to their destinations; they are quite compact and can traverse buildings as well as climb steep inclines.
One sees clearly in this drawing the manner by which

83. *Otto, City of the Future.* No. 83.

Perspective sketch, 1963
Pencil on light board, 11¾ x 15¾" (29.8 x 40.0 cm.)
Signed: "Frei Otto 1963"
Lent by Frei Otto

buildings and platforms are suspended from high masts, which allows a building to be built literally from the top down. A series of tensile roofs provides varying degrees of shelter for public spaces beneath. These translucent membranes trap radiant heat while protecting the ground below. There is no clear distinction between inside and outside spaces, and indeed the beehive-like quality of Otto's visionary urban fabric relies strongly on the complete integration of a complex web of circulation systems. All functions are interconnected, and—as with many visionary urban schemes—there is a lack of area in the private domain.

84   Major Urban Concentration Between a Lake and the Sea, bird's-eye view

Perspective sketch, 1963
Pencil on light board, 11¾ x 15¾" (29.8 x 40.0 cm.)
Signed: "Frei Otto '63"
Lent by Frei Otto

This sketch gives an impression of a city of the future which has been built along a populous coastal region. Motor traffic is confined to an outlying belt system, and internal circulation is carried on a suspended system of rails that transports passengers between peripheral carparks and their destinations. Service vehicles move underground or use a system of canals. Immense masts support a dense network of tension cables off of which buildings can be hung. All the functions and services of a complete city are contained within this lattice that envisions an intertwining of terrace-like building complexes. Density is insured by the pedestrian scale and by a complete three-dimensional integration of all functions.
On the shore of a lake, to the right, is a large pneumatic structure, which contains a year-round bathing beach and a small evergreen recreational park. To the lower left is a sports stadium where the grandstands are protected by a hung tensile structure that anticipates somewhat Otto's dramatic roofs for the stadia at the XX Olympics at Munich.

Thomas Anderson

Born of an architectural engineer father and of a mother eager for space, this double heredity, faced in turn with the existence of an older brother as Inspector General of Historic Monuments of France and a sister as a classic dancer, makes this architect a being eternally teetering between the strict discipline of cogitative reasoning and the imperious demands of lyricism.
After a poor show in his preparatory studies for l'Ecole Polytechnique and an even more miserable performance at the Paris Beaux Arts, he found a bit of joy working with Le Corbusier. But his most important encounter was with the artists of the 1950s, thanks to André Bloc and the magazine l'Architecture d'Aujourd'hui. He frequently saw Arp, Fernand Léger, Sonia Delaunay, Agam, Tinguely, Soto, Dewasne, Pillet, Armand, César, Gilioli, Bury, Vasarely and worked often with them on projects of architecture and the integration of the arts. This provided his formation.
But the most important encounter occurred in 1964 with the master glass maker Paul Virilio. From it came the hypothesis of the "Fonction Oblique" and the nine issues of the manifesto architecture principe.
Claude Parent finds in the oblique the response to all his concerns about introducing implicit movement into architecture. His Drusch villa dating from 1963 already announced his deliberate abandonment of orthogonal forms (Maison de l'Iran, 1961-68) for forms in equilibrium visually utilizing the vacillation of masses (Eglise de Nevers, 1964).
Two prestigious masters have always guided the architect in his course and in his endeavours. Frank Lloyd Wright, whose Guggenheim Museum seems to him to be one of the only seeds of the future, and Mendelsohn. The realization that is most precious to him is the Centre Commercial of Sens (1970) with its immense ramps plying amongst the boutiques.

Perspective sketch, "Dec. '65"
Pencil on tracing paper, 27⅜ x 40⅛" (69.5 x 102.0 cm.)
Signed: "C. Parent"
Lent by Claude Parent

85   "Les Vagues—I" (The Waves—I), overview   *(fig. 84)*

86   "Les Enroulés—II" (The Encoiled—II), overview
(fig. 42)

Perspective rendering, May, 1967
Pencil and felt-tip pen on tracing paper, 30½ x 42⅝" (77.5 x 108.2 cm.)
Signed: "C. Parent 1.5.67"
Lent by Claude Parent

Les Vagues (The Waves)
These oblique urban structures, inclined to the ground, advance in successive waves following the motion of the ocean. They surround space in their rhythmic correspondence of one to the other.
Inside, the floors are all inclined; their continuous undulation determines the habitable (private) spaces. Their structuring of space corresponds to the theory of "Fonction Oblique" which requires the substitution of horizontal and vertical planes (orthogonal order) by a linkage of ramps and counter ramps (oblique order).
This architecture, urbanism, and the resulting disposition of space are in violent opposition to the two classic territorial allocations: the horizontal (village—Los Angeles), the vertical (cathedral—Manhattan). In oblique structure, all the planes that contribute to communication between people (circulation) or to their protection (habitation) are of use.
We arrive at two theorems about the utilization of space:
1) Habitable circulation: it is the same support structure that allows for circulation and habitation. One inhabits moving about; one moves about inhabiting—
2) The surmountable object: an inclined structure allows one to leap over that urban obstacle that is the dwelling. One does not deform it, one traverses it like a bridge. One walks on the facades.
Beginning with the spatial theme of the oblique, all forms of attacking spatial problems are conceivable.
Les Enroulés are merely a special case; *les vagues* continue to be the basic leitmotif.

Claude Parent

St. Florian, Friedrich (Graz, Austria, 1932-)

St. Florian, a registered architect and member of the American Institute of Architects, studied architecture at the Technical University in Graz, the Ecole Nationale Superieure d'Architecture in Brussels (Atelier Victor Bourgeois), and the Federal Institute of Technology of Zurich. He came to the United States as a Fulbright Fellow in 1961 and completed his graduate studies at Columbia University in 1962. He has taught architectural design at Columbia University, at the Massachusetts Institute of Technology and the Rhode Island School of Design, where he is now Dean of Architecture.
His theoretical work has been published and shown in numerous exhibitions around the world, notably in Buenos Aires, London, Milan, New York, Rome, Stockholm, Tokyo, and Vienna.
Honors include a fellowship at MIT's Center for Advanced Visual Studies, National Endowment for the Arts awards, and several prizes in national and international design competition.
His works are in the collection of the Museum of Modern Art, New York; Museum of Art, Rhode Island School of Design; MIT; and numerous private collections.

87 "City Nucleus in Space (2),"axonometric   *(fig. 85)*

City Nuclei exist at various altitudes. Such a City Nucleus would "float in space," anchored at its parameters to the vertical city and supported by centrally located vertical circulation systems.
The City Nuclei are analogous to the public spaces of historic cities. There would be public gardens with the flora planned to correspond to varying altitudes (from common plants to alpine flora in the upper regions). Such a city nucleus would contain all functions that pertain to public city life: government functions, offices, theaters, concert halls, restaurants, shops, galleries, entertainment.

The Vertical City, a Project, 1964-66
There are two historical links to the notion of a vertical city. From a rational point of view such a concept could be seen as a logical continuation (transformation, perhaps) of the linear city idea of the late 19th and early 20th centuries. It is certainly the continuation of one of mankind's most ardent dreams—to build beyond the clouds and to challenge the skies.
The Tower of Babel, the Eiffel Tower, Frank Lloyd Wright's Mile-high Skyscraper are all testimony to this temptation. A technological triumph perhaps, but more importantly a monument to man's will to build tall.

88 The Vertical City, axonometric   *(fig. 38)*

Rendering, 1964-66
Ink and pencil on white roll paper, 9½' x 3' (2 m. 89.8 cm. x 90.5 cm.)
Unsigned
Lent by Friedrich St. Florian

Society seldom looks favorably at such attempts. Only moments of great outward thrust—such as the early and mid-sixties—allow so extravagant a thought: to build a tower, a city, so tall that it would penetrate the median altitude of cloud covers over North America, thus adding at least 100 more days of unobstructed sunshine to its uppermost portions. In these regions beyond the clouds would be situated those segments of societal activities that would most benefit: hospitals, schools, homes for the elderly. Solar energies could be harvested almost daily at this

85.   *St. Florian, City Nucleus in Space.* No. 87.

Study rendering, "1963, Providence, R.I."
Pencil on tracing paper, 28 x 29"   (71.1 x 73.7 cm.)
Unsigned
Lent by Friedrich St. Florian

outreach beyond the clouds.
To build a vertical city of such magnitude (approximately
300 stories) is not impossible structurally. The basic
cylindrical shape for the structural components reflects the
concern for engineering efficiency.
At intervals—not unlike the models of a linear city—there
are interchanges; one at the base of the city, another on the
top.

89 City Crown, axonometric

Rendering, 1964-66
Ink and pencil on drawing board 39½ x 25¾" (100.3 x 65.4
cm.)
Unsigned
Lent by Friedrich St. Florian

Airborne modes of transportation, short haul VTOs (Vertical
Take-Offs), and helicopter services interchange with the
vertical modes of transportation. The city crown also serves as
a mammoth solar energy collector and communication center.
Schools, hospitals, homes for the elderly are in close
proximity to the city crown.

Friedrich St. Florian

Sant'Elia, Antonio (Como, Italy, 1888—Monfalcone, Italy, 1916)

Sant'Elia was the only major Italian architectural talent of the generation of Gropius, Le Corbusier, and Mies van der Rohe. He worked and studied in Milan from 1905; competition projects with Paternoster (Monza Cemetery), Cantoni (Milan Central Station), and others. There is only one building known by his own hand: Villa Elisi, San Maurizio, Como, 1911. He was a founder member of the group "Nuove Tendenze," 1912, with whom he exhibited "Città Nuova" drawings in May 1914. Taken up by F.T. Marinetti and Futurists; his "Messaggio sull'Architettura Moderna" from the Nuove Tendenze catalogue was reissued in altered form as "Manifesto dell'Architettura Futurista" in July 1914. After Sant'Elia's death—he was killed in action in World War I—his reputation was cultivated by Marinetti who made the "Città Nuova" drawings and manifesto known in avant-garde circles in Europe and Russia. These had a discernible (if slight) influence on the early International Style architecture and urbanism of Le Corbusier, Neutra, et al., but his reputation waned outside Italy where it became an increasingly provincial (not to say, fascist) affair until the sudden world-wide revival of interest in 1955; since then Sant'Elia has been recognized as one of the fundamental architectural visionaries of the present century.

90 "Città Nuova" (New City), stepped building with elevators from the four street floors, perspective elevation   *(fig. 12)*

Rendering, 1914
Black ink and pencil on paper, 22 x 21⅝" (56 x 55 cm.)
Stamped: "Antonio Sant'Elia, architetto. S. Raffaele, No. 3, Milano"
Lent by Avv. Paride Accetti, Milan

Sant'Elia's carefully prepared perspectives of the "Città Nuova," or "Milano 2000," stand in the tradition of urban restructuring that goes back through Hénard, Moilin, and Paxton's Crystal Way, but also pick up the new vitality given such visions by the science fiction of H.G. Wells and others. Recognized since their first publication as constituting one of the most compelling images of the twentieth-century city, they have been influential in their parts and their totality. As early as 1921 the characteristic format of stepped-back apartments with vertical elevators was taken over by Henri Sauvage (rue des Amiraux, Paris); and as late as 1962-72 an even more literal rendering was produced by Sir Leslie Martin and Patrick Hodgkinson (Brunswick Centre, London). Incorporation after 1955 into the lectures and writings of members of the international planning establishment, like Percy Johnson-Marshall, gave these drawings a second lease on life as the inspiration of a whole series of multi-level high density urban designs, from Cumbernauld Town Center in Scotland, to most of the proposals to "do something about Manhattan" since about 1964.

91 "La Centrale Elettrica" (Central Electric Power Station), elevation   *(fig. 86)*

Though dated 1914, this colored presentation drawing (apparently intended as a gift to Sant'Elia's admirer, Mario Bugelli) reverts to the freer and more decorative sketching style he had used in 1912 (contrast the tight and controlled draughtsmanship of La Città Nuova, no. 90). Electrical generating stations were a favorite literary theme in Futurist circles, for whom they were an image of the clean new power that freed men from slavery to their past. Sant'Elia here realizes the theme in the richest, most dramatic, and most ornate of all his many renderings—a resounding image of the monumental power of the new technology, to which the thin

86. *Sant' Elia, Central Electric Power Station.* No. 91.

Perspective sketch, "Como, 25/2/1914"
Black, green, and red ink, and black pencil on paper, 12¼ x 8⅛"
(31 x 20.5 cm.)
Unsigned
Lent by Avv. Paride Accetti, Milan

tracery of the smoke rising from the stacks gives a surprising
Art Nouveau grace-note, almost in the manner of C.R.
Mackintosh.

Reyner Banham

Scharoun, Hans (Bremen, 1893—Berlin, 1972)

Among the Expressionist architects of post World War I, Hans Scharoun is notable in that he was able to carry out important large buildings after World War II in that same city of Berlin that was the setting of so much fervor and visionary dreaming around 1920. In Scharoun's buildings and projects the organic architecture of Expressionism comes full circle after the decisive interlude of the International Style and the shattering years of political dictatorship and war.

Scharoun grew up in Bremerhaven, a busy international port in those days; after studying architecture at the Technische Hochschule Berlin-Charlottenburg, he spent 1915-1918 with the army in East Prussia in its department of reconstruction. After the war, he did not return to architectural school, but stayed on in Insterburg, East Prussia, engaged in architectural work and presenting projects in competitions. He became a member of Die "Gläserne Kette" (The Glass Chain) and in 1926 joined "Der Ring" to which Mies van der Rohe, Häring, Poelzig, Mendelsohn, Hilberseimer, and the brothers Taut also belonged. Scharoun went to Breslau to teach at the Staatliche Akademie für Kunst und Kunstgewerbe, and while in Breslau he participated in the Weissenhof-Siedlung, Stuttgart, 1927, organized by the Werkbund and under the artistic direction of Mies van der Rohe. In 1932, he had begun work on Berlin's Siemensstadt housing, and he chose to live in the Siemensstadt and ride out the Nazi storm, building a few private houses and creating much work on paper. Two of the drawings in this exhibition date from those years, while the others were done just after World War I in Insterburg.

After 1945, Hans Scharoun was an influential figure on the German architectural scene. He received many honors. His projects in architectural competitions often won first place, and—most importantly—he saw a number of major buildings actually built. Of the latter, in Berlin, the Philharmonic Concert Hall, 1963, and the Staatsbibliothek, still in construction, sum up ideas about architectural space and form as the setting for the meaningful social interaction of people, which were basic to Scharoun's philosophy throughout his life.

92 Untitled drawing: Kulthaus?, elevation *(fig. 6)*

Watercolor sketch, 1919
Watercolor on smooth cardboard, 18¾ x 14¼" (47.6 x 36 cm.)
Unsigned
Lent by Akademie der Künste, Berlin, Sammlung Baukunst, Scharoun Archiv

The themes of "Kulthaus" (cultural center) and of "Volkshaus" (community center) occurred over and over again in the writings and drawings of the Expressionists. Scharoun did numerous versions, and often it is impossible to say, as in this watercolor of 1919, which of the two or if perhaps a combination of both is meant. Following the Expressionists' call for an architecture of color and glass, Scharoun placed his joyous vision, wrapped in a burst of light, onto an older grey townscape. In a Sittesque manner, irregular streets open onto a glorious public building which is fitted into the existing urban context. The pointed arches of Scharoun's vision carry the Gothic into the indeterminate future.
Scharoun's watercolors of this period were stylistically very much part of the Expressionist movement, especially its graphic work. Although he never seems to have thought of himself as anything but an architect, he chose a medium and style to express his scheme for buildings in a utopian future that had little to do with the draughting room.

93 Untitled drawing of walled city, elevation

Watercolor sketch, 1919
Watercolor on smooth cardboard, 9⅞ x 14" (25.1 x 35.5 cm.)
Unsigned
Lent by Akademie der Künste, Berlin, Sammlung Baukunst, Scharoun Archiv

Like the other watercolor in the exhibition, this one dates from the crucial year 1919, when the young generation of artists and architects was filled with fervent hopes for a better and peaceful future, and was bound together by their ardent dreams.
Scharoun's architectural vision here is part of a city, or perhaps it is a whole city, that we glimpse like a forbidden land through a break in the slightly convex red wall. From pointed spires a star-shaped halo of light covers the sky, while cold blue shadows fall outside the wall.

87.   *Scharoun, Untitled Drawing.* No. 94.

Sketch, 1939-45
Pen and wash on thin paper, 8¼ x 11¾" (20.9 x 29.7 cm.)
Unsigned
Lent by Akademie der Künste, Berlin, Sammlung Baukunst,
Scharoun Archiv

Compositionally this is a complete picture set into a frame and a design of balance and symmetry. We are drawn into the center through the gate to the shining communal building—cathedral, art center, people's palace, skyscraper(?).

94 Untitled drawing of building with floors, elevation   *(fig. 87)*

This drawing—one of those Scharoun did during the years 1939-45—represents an open-air performance scenario. There is no real stage, however, nor visible distinction between performers and public: all are participants in some grand communal act.
Scharoun's preoccupation with the movement of people through architectural multilevel spaces, evident in many drawings from these years, may hark back to early impressions of the port of his hometown. Tiny figures populate these schemes, indicating scale as well as movement. This multi-level structure with its bridges daringly cantilevered into space and connected by a narrow walk-way above the enormous stairs has a nautical character, especially if the flowing shapes to either side and above the central space are suspended sails. Sails or wings, this somewhat threatening structure sits like an animate object in a desolate landscape.

95 Untitled drawing of building with wings, elevation

Sketch, 1939-45
Pencil on thin paper, 9 x 9" (22.9 x 22.9 cm.)
Unsigned
Lent by Akademie der Künste, Berlin, Sammlung Baukunst, Scharoun Archiv
In this pencil drawing, as in its companion from this later group of wartime works on paper, people are ascending steps to a monumental structure. Tiny figures on the curved roof seem to indicate that this is a sculpture rather than a building to be entered. As in Scharoun's later and actually built Berlin Philharmonic, the flow and movement of people clarifies and complements architectural form and space, and becomes an integral part of the performance.
Behind the opening between the winglike shapes rise faintly-drawn twin towers. This structural complex could be floating in space. No setting is indicated. Are we witnessing the take-off for a flight into outer space?

Christiane C. Collins

Paolo Soleri was born and raised in Torino, where he was educated and received his doctorate in architecture in 1947. He then came to America and worked for Frank Lloyd Wright at the two Taliesins. Two years later he went back to Italy where, near Salerno, he built a large ceramics factory, Ceramica Artistica Solimene. In 1954 Soleri returned to the U.S., where he settled and now lives in Scottsdale, Arizona. There he organized the Cosanti Foundation in 1956 which produces beautiful ceramic and metal bells and plans the building of Arcosanti. Projected to be an arcology or urban habitat for some 3,000 people, Arcosanti has been since 1965 the major ongoing building project for Soleri. Starting with his "Cosmic Potentials" plan in 1950, but especially since 1956, Soleri has produced a steady flow of visionary megastructures, including his "Mesa Cities" (1958-1962), "Arcologies" (1967-), and "3-D Jersey" (1968). Soleri continues to design, build, lecture, and write. Among his most recent major projects is the "Two Suns Arcology," a revision of Arcosanti that makes extensive use of solar energy.

96 "The Six Suns, a High Density Tower," plans, elevations, details *(fig. 7)*

Study sketches, August 1960
Crayon on butcher paper, 48 x 281¾" (1.22 m. x 7.156 m.)
Scale: 1 cm. = 25 m.
Signed twice: "p.v. [Paradise Valley] Agusto [August] 1960
Paolo Soleri"
Lent by the Cosanti Foundation, Scottsdale, Arizona

This series of three sketches is one of Soleri's Mesa City projects, a megastructure designed as a city and total environment for two million people in an area roughly the size of Manhattan. Mesa City was Soleri's first attempt at organizing a concentrated urban system within a single complex.

Sketch 1   This sketch shows just the lower elements of the Six Suns tower. Light and radiant heat from six artificial suns mounted in the crown of the tower help create an environment suitable for lush vegetation, parks, and even bathing beaches along a circumferential lagoon. Most of the industries are automated and located below ground level. The concentration of population and the containment of pollution called for in Soleri's schemes will preserve and protect the natural environment. Soleri feels that this increased concentration leads to greater cultural complexity that, in itself, increases the potential of man. Although this structure rises in the air, the scheme remains basically horizontal, since transportation and services remain at ground level. Soleri has since come to concentrate more activities above ground.

Sketch 2   The plan of the Six Suns Mesa City at ground level is shown here. The structure consists of six immense buttresses forming the shape of a star around which a lagoon can be seen. Paolo Soleri has described himself as a sun worshiper, and this in part accounts for his reliance on the atomic generating heat plants described as the six suns of these drawings, as well as some of the inspiration for his graphic style. Sketches such as this one and those to the right inevitably invite comparisons to organic forms, and indeed, so much is unspecified in his drawings that they can be appreciated solely on a compositional level.

Sketch 3   This series shows a nearly complete elevation of the Six Suns Mesa City, a sketch of the plan, an elevation of the top platform that houses the six suns, and a schematic sketch of the transportation systems that bind together the lower levels of the city. The arched buttresses of the base support a central core around which are cantilevered hundreds of floors of dwellings. Three more of these immense mushrooming highrises can be seen in the distance at the lower right. The degree of social cooperation necessary to create a Mesa City makes these projects clearly utopian. The architect intends to reorder the social and cultural life of every citizen into a new harmony. Indeed, in the last chapter of his book *Matter Becoming Spirit*, he often uses the term "Civitate Dei" ("City of God") to describe his projects.[76]

97   Cantilever Bridge, elevation   *(fig. 33)*

Study sketch, 1962
Crayon and ink on butcher paper, 48 x 188¾" (1.22 m. x 4.79 m.)
Signed: "1962 PROOF Paolo Soleri"
Lent by the Cosanti Foundation, Scottsdale, Arizona

This drawing shows a sinuous single cantilever construction spanning from 1,800 to 2,300 feet. Running through this assemblage of muscular material, probably reinforced concrete, is a highway with access ramps that wind down through the structure. The free and vigorous strokes of crayon and ink wash indicate the thoroughly intuitive manner of its design. Bridges have held a long fascination for Soleri. One of his most famous bridges was his first, the Tube Bridge, a continuous folded tube of concrete, designed while Soleri was working for Frank Lloyd Wright. His greatest bridge designing activity was in 1962, the date of this drawing, when he designed and built models of many bridge projects such as the Arch Beam Bridge, the Plow Bridge, and the Centrifugal Bridge. Soleri is not trained as an engineer and none of his bridge projects have been realized, yet his work is endlessly inventive and provocative. Soleri described his method as "a graphic abstraction enlivened by an organic propensity."[77]

98 'Arcology—Babel' Babel II B and Asteromo II, plans, elevations, sections   *(fig. 88)*

The arcologies were the next major phase in the development of Soleri's megastructures.

Sketch 1   Arcology Babel II B is an immense vision of the future with eight of the architect's characteristic stalk-like towers joined at tower and base. His arcology projects number over forty, and on a formal level they are quite flexible. Yet the same basic ideas about urban habitat remain essentially unchanged. Among these constants are the complete integration of mechanization into everyday life, a tightly knit, interdependent and cooperative society, and an almost complete isolation of man's habitat from nature with "Cosmodomes" enclosing microclimates and artificial suns, forming a highly defined boundary between man and nature. Soleri's work has often been compared with that of Buckminster Fuller because both have faith in the ultimate utopian potential of technology.

Sketch 2   Shown here are a longitudinal and a transverse section of Asteromo II, a spaceship with artificial gravity provided by slow rotation. Soleri's vision of total environmental control within the context of a high degree of social organization makes his arcologies well suited as space colonies. Shaped like an open lattice watermelon, the peripheral areas are devoted to agriculture and solar collection. Public life is built around the center, where gravity is least, and the environment is most stable. Powered by atomic and solar energy, Asteromo is a totally self-sufficient environment.

Sketch 3   This is a section through two towers that form the width of the Arcology Babel II B. These towers support a multileveled platform that contains cultural amenities. The towers themselves contain housing. Within the lattices of the carefully structured habitat, the individual owner determines the facade and model of his dwelling unit. The archidome is the opaque boundary of arcology over the parklands surrounding the base and provides the first zone of climatic control. Between the towers is a large gymnasium and more facilities for recreation. Automated industries, factories, and utilities are all subterranean, and on the ground level are parks and hills with large air conditioning vents. The "panoramic road" is a circumferential highway that links the radiating transportation links to other arcologies. Within the central core below ground level is an atomic energy generating plant, drawn as an orange ball which can be either fission or fusion as technology and means allow.

Sketch 4   This large sketch is a blowup of the upper platform of the Babel II B, to the left. The structure is seen to be a forest of heroic buttresses and tension arms that support the cantilevered platforms. Springing over the whole is a dome that protects the microenvironment of parks, while underneath this platform a radiant heat dish beams down energy to the land below. Within the towers are cultural facilities and plenty of open green spaces. Parks may be seen poised beneath the webbing of structure. Horizontal transportation is largely by foot or bicycle, while elevators take one through the more than three hundred stories. The hollow central core forms an enormous skylight from which the dwellings are built on cantilevered decks.

Thomas Anderson

88.   *Soleri, Arcology-Babel (detail).* No. 98.

Study sketches, 1965-66
Crayon on butcher paper, 42" x 34½' (1.07 m. x 10.42 m.)
Scale: 1 cm = 50 m and 1 cm = 25 m
Signed: variously, "Paolo Soleri . . ."
Lent by the Cosanti Foundation, Scottsdale, Arizona

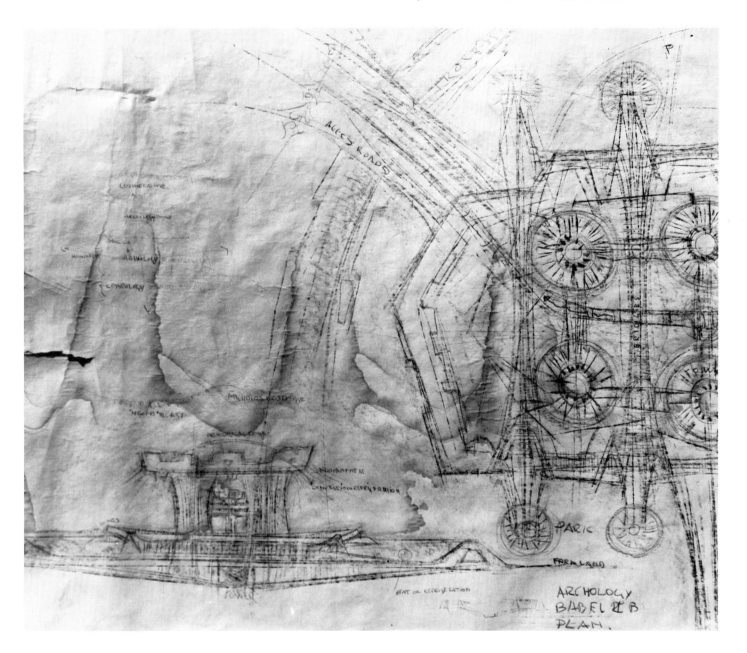

Stevens, Herbert H., Jr. (Gardiner, Maine, 1913-)

Engineer and humanist, Stevens received a degree in Mechanical Engineering from Georgia Institute of Technology in 1936 and a master's degree in Liberal Studies from the New School for Social Research in 1969. Apart from his innovations in the theory of air-supported, i.e., pneumatic, structures for which he held a very early patent, Stevens has been in positions of research and development on the design of aircraft seats, rolling steel doors, electric shavers, paint sprayers, and nuclear fuels. His intellectual interests and writings range from philosophy to the history of science and mathematics; he has published especially on Finitism, a new scientific philosophy. As an active member of the Society of Friends and of their New England Yearly Meeting, Stevens writes on social and philosophical matters for Quaker Life. *An example of the futuristic vision of his pneumatic structures was the 13-acre air-supported roof that he designed for the aircraft manufacturer Glenn L. Martin to cover a stadium that was to have been erected in Baltimore, Maryland, in 1945.*

99 Airplane Factory with air-supported roof, bird's-eye view *(fig. 89)*

100 Airplane Factory with air-supported roof, interior perspective view   *(fig. 31)*

Rendering, 1942
Charcoal on paper, 11⅜ x 19¾" (29 x 50 cm.)
Signed: "Hugh Ferriss, del."
Lent by Herbert H. Stevens, Jr.

Stevens described the project in *Architectural Record* for December 1942 (pp. 45-46): "The roof of the factory here described is a thin, steel membrane constructed with insulation and roofing flat on the ground and fastened to a concrete anchor ring. It is then raised and stretched into a dome shape by air pressure from ordinary ventilating blowers, and thereafter is supported by a pressure of one ounce per square inch from these blowers. The effect of this pressure on the occupants is negligible as it never exceeds the difference in air pressure between the top and bottom floors of a sixty story building.
"The working area within the factory is completely free of columns and other structural obstructions which interfere with production in ordinary buildings. The structure uses one tenth the amount of steel and other priority materials ordinarily used.
"The factory is well protected against air leakage. All doors are double, forming airlocks, with the exception of revolving doors for personnel and the single door where railroad trains enter. In the last case the bulk of the car fills the opening and air loss is not great. Leakage is so slight that the fans could be stopped for several days before the roof would settle seriously, and in case of shut-down periods a single relatively small fan can keep the roof supported indefinitely. . . .
"Excess pressure is always carried to prevent the roof from fluttering in the wind. The slight positive pressure exerts a damping effect that prevents ripples from starting. Since the roof is a perfect form to resist internal pressure, the suction effect of the wind on the roof is not excessive . . . .
"The danger of complete collapse is more a psychological problem than actual one. Any one of the sixteen ventilating fans comprising the ventilating system is sufficient to keep the roof inflated, and half of these are driven by gasoline engines independent of power failure. This extra capacity is

89. *Stevens, Airplane Factory*, No. 99.

Rendering, 1942
Pencil on paper, 11 x 8½" (28 x 21.5 cm.)
Labeled: "Herbert H. Stevens Jr." (with address, etc.); Hugh
Ferriss added the shading.
Lent by Herbert H. Stevens, Jr.

required to take out heat in the summer, as air lost by leakage and operation of the air locks is very slight . . . .
"The factory is easily and rapidly built and will have low overhead and upkeep costs. It is suitable for all kinds of manufacturing operations with its clear unobstructed working area. It is easy to camouflage, and suitable for 24-hour-a-day blackout."

Superstudio (founded Florence, Italy, 1966)
Adolfo Natalini (1941-), founder;
Christiano Toraldo di Francia (1941-), founder;
Roberto Magris (1935-);
Piero Frassinelli (1939-);
Alessandro Magris (1941-).

Superstudio soon rose to international fame as the most successful of the numerous groups that came out of Florence University in the mid-60s. Its founders shared the growing interest at the Architecture School in a wider role for architects through political activity, group work, the development of technology, and large scale projects. The influence of the English school, and particularly of Archigram, was fundamental. The abstraction of Superstudio's first work "A journey into the realm of reason" and its machine-like entries for several competitions made clear from the beginning the dual aspect of its activities: on one side a positivistic view of architecture as the final act of reason and a means of changing the world, expressed through theoretical work and powerful images; on the other side their parallel professional activity (bank renovations, private homes, etc.). In "Istogrammi d'architettura" (1969) Superstudio's research became more abstract: in its study of pure geometry, "Platonic entities," this work came closer to the permutations of Sol LeWitt than to previous projects. With the Italian economic crisis Superstudio's work grew more cynical, more fatalistic ("Monumento Continuo," 1970), and relied on extremely refined graphics; the projects became didactic: "the image as communication." In "Interplanetary Architecture" (1971), no sign is left of the initial optimism: the imagery becomes self-criticism, acknowledgment of the frustrations of architects. Only a new interplanetary architecture will liberate men from the "rational logic of architecture as production of consumer goods." In 1972, for the Museum of Modern Art show "Italy, The New Domestic Landscape," Superstudio presented "Life Education Ceremony Love Death" a series of films on the fundamental acts of life. In them architecture is condemned for not dealing with the great themes of our life, the architect being "an accomplice to the machinations of the system." The redefining of relationships between architecture and the fundamental acts of life is indicated as the only path to salvation.
More recently Superstudio has been involved with education, and, together with other members of the Italian avant garde, has founded the Global Tools, a workshop for the study of industrial elements.

101 "On the River," perspective view *(fig. 90)*

102 "St. Moritz Revisited," perspective panorama *(fig. 37)*

Photomontage, 1969
Collage and pencil on paper, 26 x 28" (66 x 96.5 cm.)
Signed: "Superstudio" on mat
Lent by the Gilman Paper Co.

The two works are part of the "Continuous Monument" which stands at midpoint in Superstudio's creative career; it is subtitled "An Architectural Model for Total Urbanization."
Tracing back to the beginning of history, man's monuments stand as reminders of his constant search for order. Stonehenge, the Kaaba, the Pyramids, the Chinese Wall are the prelude to the total urbanization of the future, created with a single act, from a single design. The Continuous Monument is the final and inevitable act of mankind, the "realization of cosmic order on earth." Refusing the mirages and temptations of spontaneous architecture and the demagogical picturesque, Superstudio bows to the power of "technology, culture and the other inevitable forms of imperialism." Rejecting any compromise, the architecture of the future will stand as the only alternative to nature: "Between the terms Natura Naturans and Natura Naturata we choose the latter." Floating over lakes, mountains, and cities, the "Continuous Monument" will house the entire population of the world. Passing over Manhattan, it embraces the Wall Street skyscrapers as souvenirs of the past chaos.
Compared to other linear cities, such as Mitchell and Boutwell's "Comprehensive City," stretching on a straight line from New York to San Francisco, the "Continuous Monument" achieves a greater degree of visionary power. Its metaphoric imagery resembles more the contemporary Land Art than the architectural utopias of the past.

Peter Marangoni

90.   *Superstudio, "On the River."* No. 101.

Photomontage, 1969
Collage and pencil on paper, 25¾ x 38" (65.5 x 96.5 cm.)
Signed: "Superstudio" on mat
Lent by the Gilman Paper Co.

Tyng, Anne Griswold (Kuling, Kiangsi, China, 1920-)

Tyng received her A.B. from Radcliffe (1942) and was one of the first women to receive the M.Arch. from Harvard Graduate School of Design, where her teachers included Gropius and Breuer. She earned her Ph.D. in Architecture (1975) at the University of Pennsylvania, where she has been Lecturer in Architecture since 1968. In 1945, she joined the office of Stonorov and Kahn in Philadelphia, and in 1947, when Louis I. Kahn established his separate office, she joined his firm, associating with him as a principal architect on a number of architectural and planning projects.

Her independent research in forming principles, for which she received a Graham Foundation grant in 1965 (published as "Geometric Extensions of Consciousness" in Zodiac 19, Milan, Italy, 1969), proposes specific links between psyche and matter. Tyng is a Fellow of the A.I.A., associate member (elect) of the National Academy of Design, member of the C.G. Jung Foundation of New York, President and founding member of the C.G. Jung Center of Philadelphia, and co-founder of Form Forum of Philadelphia, an interdisciplinary group centered at the University of Pennsylvania.

103 Urban Hierarchy: Bilateral and Rotational Symmetries, plans *(fig. 34a)*

Diagrams with explanations, 1970
Pencil, ink, magic marker and typing on white tracing paper, 8½ x 11" (21.5 x 28 cm.)
Unsigned
Lent by Anne Griswold Tyng

104 Urban Hierarchy: Helical Symmetry (Randomized), plan *(fig. 34b)*

Diagram with explanation, 1970
Pencil, ink, magic marker, and typing on white tracing paper, 8½ x 11" (21.5 x 28 cm.)
Unsigned
Lent by Anne Griswold Tyng

105 Urban Hierarchy: Spiral Symmetry, plan *(fig. 34c)*

Diagram with explanation, 1970
Pencil, ink, magic marker, typing on white tracing paper, 8½ x 11" (21.5 x 28 cm.)
Unsigned
Lent by Anne Griswold Tyng

106 Urban Hierarchy: Large-scale bilateral symmetry, plan *(fig. 34d)*

Diagram with explanation, 1970
Pencil, ink, magic marker, and typing on white tracing paper, 8½ x 11" (21.5 x 28 cm.)
Unsigned
Lent by Anne Griswold Tyng

107 Spiral Urban Hierarchy, drawing for model *(fig. 91)*

108 Spiral Urban Hierarchy: Bird's-eye drawing for detail model

Sketched overview, 1970
Charcoal on yellow tracing paper, 11 x 11" (28 x 28 cm.)
Unsigned
Lent by Anne Griswold Tyng

Bird's-eye sketch, 1970
Charcoal on yellow tracing paper, 12 x 20" (30.5 x 51 cm.)
Unsigned
Lent by Anne Griswold Tyng

An exploration of a 20th-Century Matrix
This urban hierarchy is based on a geometric matrix similar to the Gothic Master Diagram. The Gothic "irrational" proportions of 5- and 10-fold symmetries are included in this 20th-Century Matrix as well as "rational" 2- and 4-fold symmetries, with 20-fold symmetry encompassing and integrating all the basic symmetries and resolving systems of proportion previously perceived as incompatible.

In the 20th century we have uncovered secret geometries of psyche and matter. We have found roots of symbolic form in the subjective geometry of "mandalas," in archetypal images of the unconscious mind. We have perceived the objective geometries of atomic bonds, helical molecules, spiralling plants and proportional growth, new laws of light and matter. In these discoveries a correlation of geometries has led me to suggest that atom, molecule, psyche, and matter are all linked by a universal forming matrix of simultaneous randomness and order based on a Fibonacci-Divine Proportion matrix.[78] This extraordinary correlation can be seen in the universal principles occurring in natural, forming processes of evolution, in laws of probability, in proportional laws of sensation—of light, sound, weight, smell, and taste,[79] in angles of vision and in the shifting phases of archetypal form empathy which fire our creative processes. We no longer need to consider "systems of proportion as incompatible with creative processes."[80] It is precisely how we perceive proportional systems that determines their significance, whether subjectively or objectively, whether as natural forming principle or objective tool, whether as numinous archetypal symbol or as dogmatic canon. Viewed as a result of probability in three-dimensional space, the geometry of proportion can be understood as a universal matrix. This 20th-Century Matrix can also be expressed mathematically as a Fibonacci-Divine Proportion numerical matrix (1, 1, 2, 3, 5, 8, 13, 21, 34, 55, 89, 144, 233, . . .) a summation series in which each number is the sum of the two preceding numbers, and which, by its 12th number (144) becomes both a summation and logarithmic series, both dimension and area, with the ratios between successive terms achieving a degree of precision in a Divine Proportion progression (i.e. $233/144 = 1.61805 . . .$, the Divine Proportion being $1.61803 . . .$). Within this probability matrix, I have found that the equilateral triangle, the pentagon, and the square were formed by laws of close-packing in Fibonacci ratios, the equilateral triangle a fitting of 3 in 5, the pentagon a fitting of 5 in 8, and the square a fitting of (4 x 2)8 in 13.[81] The equilateral triangle, square, and pentagon are the only three faces that occur in the Five Platonic Solids, the only regular polyhedrons possible in three-dimensional space. These five solids and their helical and spiral extensions are the three-dimensional Fibonacci-Divine Proportional Matrix.

Such a 20th-Century Matrix can reconnect and integrate our orthogonally ordered cities with the more dynamic symmetries of helical and spiral movement systems. New possibilities of movement on ground and in the air have stretched our perceptions to speeding and air-view imagery. The vitality of these images, the interlacing geometry of expressway interchange, can happily join and relieve the scaleless spread of orthogonal gridiron.

Based on a 20th-Century Matrix, this Urban Hierarchy is one attempt to explore a unified field theory of scales, symmetries, of movement systems, of technologies, and of thresholds of identity between the individual and the largest collective scale. In applying this theory to the building of collective form, simultaneity of symmetries connects rectilinear form to pentagonal, decagonal, helical, and spiral order and again to rectilinear or bilateral form at larger scale, including complexity within simplicity. Layering of symmetries is correlated with shifts of scale. Incremental distinctions are made between static and dynamic form as steps between the architecture of place and the architecture of movement. This simultaneity of symmetries, scales, and movement systems is further correlated with a distinction between high and low technologies and their recombination. The low technology of a wall-bearing, 2- or 3-story house retains its structural identity within the high-technology terrain of street-platform and utility support structure and occurs as one threshold of identity from house to court cluster, to "hill village," to elementary school neighborhood, to junior and senior high school community and to the commercial crossroads aligned with the expressway interchange. Spanning of high density forms for horizontal connection provides public/private interface for each house, "defensible space" with access for police car, ambulance, and fire truck.

Bilateral symmetry is the basis of a court block of forty dwelling units arranged in a rectangular form. Pedestrian-park crossovers within the rectangle provide a central neighborhood meeting place. The principle of street access to and parking under each house diffuses traffic so that the street once more becomes a friendly place.

Rotational symmetry, or symmetry around a point, expresses the pattern of vehicular movement in the form of pentagonal ramps. A double helix is formed by two interlocking pentagonal ramps, one up and one down, which provide access to the units. Helical symmetry forms the "hill villages" which contain day care, Head Start, and incidental shopping facilities. Clusters of six or more helices with more random connective patterns comprise an elementary school neighborhood with supermarket shopping and other community facilities.

Spiral symmetry connects the elementary school neighborhoods to the larger community around two junior high schools and a senior high, with additional shopping, offices, motels, amusement or recreational facilities, community services, and institutions. The top level of the spiral form may be planted and used as a park-promenade, for outdoor exhibits, parades, and festivities, providing another link at the larger collective scale of the development. The expanding or contracting curve of the spiral speeds or slows traffic between house and expressway.

Bilateral symmetry at a larger scale includes four spiral forms which act as collectors and diffusers of the expressway system, with multi-level roadways forming exits and entrances to a high-speed system. The spirals offer a generating form for further growth and population expansion. This large-scale inclusion of spiral complexity within bilateral simplicity reaffirms the basic bilateral symmetry of the human body.

The numinous power of geometry and proportional systems throughout history suggests that they are fundamental links between psyche and matter—the great objective-subjective connectors of systems and symbols, natural processes and human creativity.[82] In the inner space of human thought patterns and their physical connectivity, and in space outside the brain, a universal 20th-Century Matrix can function as a "mandala" of symbolic psychic source and as a specific objective tool for the making of collective form in architecture.

Anne Griswold Tyng

Wachsmann, Konrad (Frankfurt, a. d. O., 1901-)

After apprenticeship as cabinet-maker and carpenter, Wachsmann studied with architects Heinrich Tessenow and Hans Poelzig, winning a Prix de Rome in 1932. He was involved early with prefabrication and, in 1942 in the United States where he had immigrated, he devised, in collaboration with Walter Gropius, the General Panel System, a stressed-skin plywood modular standardized house construction. He invented Mobilar Structure which was to be used in the aircraft hanger here exhibited (nos. 109, 92). He has served as professor at Illinois Institute of Technology (1949-56) and at the University of Southern California School of Architecture where he is now emeritus. Wachsmann has lectured widely throughout the world, has received honorary degrees from German and American universities, and was awarded the Gold Medal of the Senate of the Republic of Italy where he designed city and harbor development for the city of Genoa in the early 1960s. His work has been exhibited widely.

109 Airplane hangar structure on tubular space frame building system, indefinite longitudinal section *(fig. 92)*

"The problem was to develop a building system which, based on standardized elements, would permit every possible combination of construction, geometrical system, building type and span, expressed in a flexible, anonymous design. However, it was also stipulated that, once erected, such a building should be easy to dismount at any time without waste of material and that the parts should then be fit for re-use in other combinations and for other purposes as often as desired. All the building elements were to be completely prefabricated by automatic mass production methods. It was further required that the number of universal standard joints be kept to a minimum, while permitting the greatest possible variety of combinations with the corresponding structural members. Moreover, within certain limits every part had to be interchangeable with any other at any time. The building system itself was to consist solely of universal standard elements, any specially dimensioned main frame or other load-bearing element of non-standard form being avoided. It was not possible to place supports around the outside of the building. The all-around cantilever, thus necessitated, was fixed at about 150 feet."[83]

110 System idea assembled from only one type of many structure parts, upward perspective *(fig. 32)*

"Schematic sketch," 1953
Ink on tracing paper (two quarters of final rendering), 24⅜ x 88½" (62 x 224.6 cm.)
Unsigned
Lent by Konrad Wachsmann

Study of a Dynamic Structure
"Only a superficial appraisal could support the opinion that the technical-scientific approach, the consistent application of automatically-controlled, industrial production processes, and the systematic modular coordination of all building elements, parts and products, leads inevitably to monotony or, as I am continually hearing with astonishment, the total destruction of every spiritual and emotional impulse. A glimpse of the future such methods may really make possible is afforded by the following structural study, one among many.

"This study... was a preliminary investigation concerned with the problem of substituting rigid nodes for the points of connection between structural elements, in contact vertically and horizontally, and with the problem of breaking down columns into groups of spatially developed elements jointed midway between two horizontal planes formed by the structural members. The distance between the point of connection of such a structural member and the axis of a group of column elements was to be determined by stress considerations.

"One aspect of the problem was to design a single, universal structural element, which, industrially produced from a material to be determined in the course of the investigations from loading conditions and production requirements, could be used in building construction for every conceivable purpose."[84]

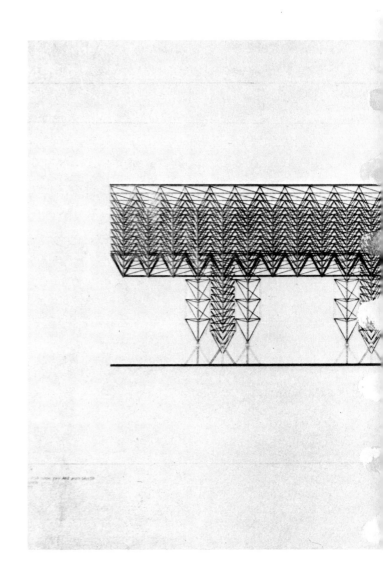

Rendering, 1951
Ink on tracing paper (only one half of rendering), 28 x 60" (71.1 x
152.4 cm.)
Unsigned. Rendering is by Pao-Chi Chang
Lent by Konrad Wachsmann

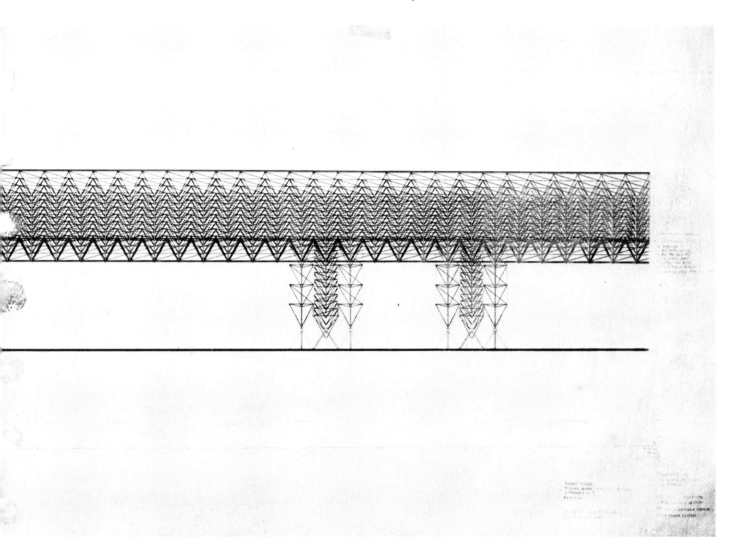

Webb, Michael David (Henley-on-Thames, England, 1937-)

"Shy, and the loner of the group," Peter Cook said of me. Well, I do like to sit at home and draw best of all, with a good movie on my drawing-board-mounted TV set. I like Elton John, Schubert, and Webern. Someone else told me I was "self-obsessed."*
To describe the project in the exhibition, I have to be sympathetic to the me that produced it. A different me. Probably, I think I loved machines, moving parts, aeroplanes (the trailing edge flaps and how they fold out when landing), drive ins . . . and inflatables . . .
because once you accepted the notion that an inflatable could be a building then you had to completely rethink such concepts as door, window, ceiling, etc. (see phases A1-B4 in exhibited drawing).
This is the me that made this drawing—just like a schoolboy, when he passionately draws two fighters locked in a midair collision, he makes explosion sounds. Boom, Crash. . . .
*I went hissss—phuph . . . beep . . . to make this more like a biography . . . *currently teaches at New Jersey School of Architecture and Massachusetts College of Art—lives in Manhattan.*

111 Cushicle Suitaloon, "Suitaloon for '67," sequences, long sections, and side views   *(fig. 93)*

dedication: I read Reyner Banham's article "A home is not a house" and it unavoidably affected me when I made this drawing

a room	could be a room, perhaps part of a house
a little room	could be the inside of a car
an even littler room	could be the space inside a suit of clothes

the project proposes that one highly sophisticated!?[85] room could perform all the functions of house, car and suit;[86] that by strapping an outboard motor to the room, it becomes a[87] car (read Reyner Banham's article "The Great Gizmo") each suit has a plug serving a similar function to that of one's front door key. You can plug into your friend and you will both end up inside one envelope (phases A7-A10), or you can plug into any envelope (phases C1-C4), stepping out of your suit which is now part of the outside wall of the envelope (suitaloon); so the wall becomes a kind of two dimensional wardrobe.

Michael Webb

93. *Webb, Cushicle/Suitaloon.* No. 111.

Working drawings, "PROJECT 1966 REVISED 1969 THIS
DRAWING COMPOSED FROM REMAINING
FRAGMENTS"
Collage of ink, prestone, and pencil on paper, mounted on
illustration board, 19⅞ x 30" (50.5 x 76.8 cm.)
Signed: "DRAWN BY SPIDER WEBB"
Lent by Michael Webb

Weidlinger Associates (established Washington, D.C., 1949-)

This is a partnership of consulting engineers with headquarters in New York City and branch offices in Boston, Massachusetts, Portsmouth, Virginia, and Palo Alto, California. What characterizes the work of Weidlinger Associates is the interplay between their Engineering Design Division and their Applied Science Division, which has allowed them to pioneer in a number of fields in both structural engineering and applied mechanics. Their Computer Section has been of basic assistance in both structural design and research.
Weidlinger Associates has designed structures all over the world and has introduced innovations in high-rise reinforced concrete construction, pneumatic structures, earthquake design, dynamic design, liquid-elastic bodies interaction, etc. They have consulted for agencies of the United States Government, as well as American and foreign industries and governments. Among their engineered buildings are the Columbia Broadcasting System Building, the Whitney Museum, and 9 West 57 Street in New York City, No. One Main Place in Dallas, Texas, the Tour Fiat in Paris, the MEBAC Theatre in Cambridge, Massachusetts, and the United States Embassies in Athens, Baghdad, and Montevideo.

112 FLAIR, the Floating Airport, perspective air-view and perspective cutaway   *(fig. 36)*

Rendering for Popular Science *magazine, August 1970*
Gouache on board, 20 x 28⅛" (50.8 x 71.4 cm.)
Signed: Ray Pioch
Lent by Weidlinger Associates

113 FLAIR, the Floating Airport, Plan (no. 1)

Rendering, 1969
Marking pen, press type, prestone, and ink on board, 18 x 23⅞"
(45.8 x 60.7 cm.)
Scale 2" = 600'
Unsigned
Lent by Weidlinger Associates

114 FLAIR, the Floating Airport, Section (no. 4)   *(fig. 94)*

The concept of a floating platform to be used as an airport for plane-hopping from one side of the Atlantic to the other is not new; it was proposed by E. R. Armstrong almost forty years ago.
The FLAIR concept as studied by Weidlinger Associates introduces three essentially new ideas into the old concept. First, the floating platform, to be used off the coast of the United States, is anchored to the bottom of the ocean (as suggested by Dr. Richard Garwin of Columbia University) so as to be stable under any weather and sea conditions; the anchorages can go to depths of 600 or more feet, with great freedom of location for the platform. Secondly, the platform is composed of reinforced concrete "bubble" units, supporting, by means of steel columns, a flat surface high enough above the sea level never to be washed by the highest wave predictable at the site. A concrete "bubble" unit is built on the coast and towed to the exact location where it is connected to previously located "bubble" units by "vacuum chambers," in which a vacuum is created temporarily. Once the new unit is temporarily connected by suction, it is permanently connected to the previous units by concrete poured in the vacuum chambers. Thirdly, the airport infra-structure of offices, terminals, fuel deposits, etc. is all contained in a level below the platform so as to leave the platform free for the runways. The airport connection with the land has been solved in a variety of ways by means of a

Rendering, 1969
Marking pen, press type, prestone, and ink on board, 18 x 23 ⅜"
(45.8 x 60.7 cm.)
Scale: 2" = 15'
Unsigned
Lent by Weidlinger Associates

floating bridge or a floating tunnel (using the same type of construction as for the platform bubbles) and by means of a totally automated feeder plane "pipe," that would allow the feeder planes to land on the platform at very short intervals. The main motivation for the feasibility study of a floating airport off the United States coast near a city is to eliminate the air and noise pollution of urban airports and to reduce the difficult traffic problem of airport approaches. The floating airport, conceived for use off New York City on the Atlantic, would allow the total elimination of ground traffic around and through the city and, with the adoption of feeder planes, the direct connection of airports from all over the United States with FLAIR.

The platform was designed to cover an area of one thousand acres. In view of its location, the platform is ideally suited for the siting of other polluting facilities, like waste disposal plants, or facilities presenting particular risks, like nuclear reactors.

The FLAIR concept is realizable with present-day techniques and is therefore totally realistic. It was utopian in terms of its cultural and economic implications when designed in 1969.

Mario G. Salvadori

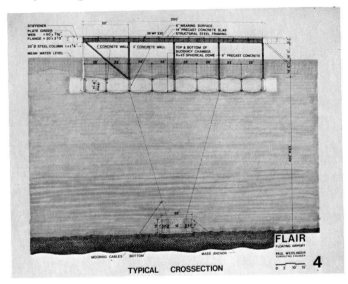

Weininger, Andrew (Karancs, Hungary, 1899-)

Educated in Pécs and Budapest, Weininger was by 1916-17 a painter of impressionist landscapes. In 1921 he went to the Bauhaus, then in Weimar, and entered Johannes Itten's basic course (see fig. 59c) and then, when the Bauhaus moved to Dessau, he entered the stage class of Oskar Schlemmer, under the influence of which he designed his famous Spherical Theater (fig. 95a). In 1922 he became attracted to the ideas of De Stijl, and Theo van Doesburg exerted a profound influence on him as we can see from his set of student drawings on exhibition—an influence that persists in his work to this day.

In 1928 Weininger left the Bauhaus and settled in Berlin as an interior architect. From 1938 to 1951, including the years of World War II, he and his wife, also trained at the Bauhaus, were in Holland. In 1951 he went to Toronto, Canada, until 1958, at which time he came to New York. He actively paints, makes reliefs and constructions, and has participated in a number of exhibitions.

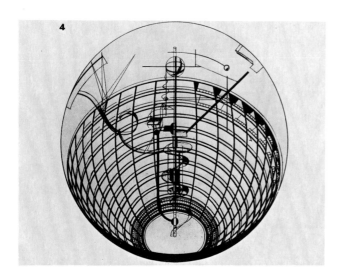

115   Half-sculptural, half-architectural design, elevations and plan   *(fig. 59a)*

School sketch (sketch on verso), 1921?
Pen and ink and pencil on paper, 5⅛ x 7⅝" (13.0 x 19.3 cm.)
Signed: "W" in red ballpoint
Lent by Andrew Weininger

116   "Fantasia house," elevation   *(fig. 59b)*

School sketch, 1922
Pencil and colored pencil on paper, 4⅜ x 4⅜" (11.2 x 11.2 cm.)
Signed: "W" in red ballpoint
Lent by Andrew Weininger

117   Rhythmical design, for Johannes Itten's class *(fig. 59c)*

School sketch, 1921
Charcoal on paper, 3¼ x 4½" (8.2 x 11.5 cm.)
Signed: "W" in red ballpoint
Lent by Andrew Weininger

118   Fantastic design for a communal building; playful forms, elevation   *(fig. 59d)*

School sketch (on verso, sketch of Hans Fuchs sitting on van de Velde lectern in Weimar Bauhaus) 1922
Pencil and watercolor on paper, 7⅞ x 7¼" (20.0 x 18.4 cm.)
Signed: "W" in red ballpoint
Lent by Andrew Weininger

"House Fantasia"
In 1922 Van Doesburg propagated the ideas of De Stijl in Weimar. I was among his followers although I was at that time a Bauhaus student with Itten. Van Doesburg was in his way no less dogmatic than Itten; for instance, the painter's field was restricted to the two-dimensional. I tried hard to find harmonious, well-balanced, abstract Stijl solutions. Contrary to the above rule, I handled this sketch in a playful way, overlapping planes, thereby extending into the three dimensional. Out of this play I tried to find out how, with puristic form elements, a Stijl architecture would look. With some additions (door, windows, balconies) I strengthened the illusion of a "house for an artist."

95. *Weininger, Spherical Theater.* Nos. 119-122 *(and photo,*
Fig. 95 *a).*

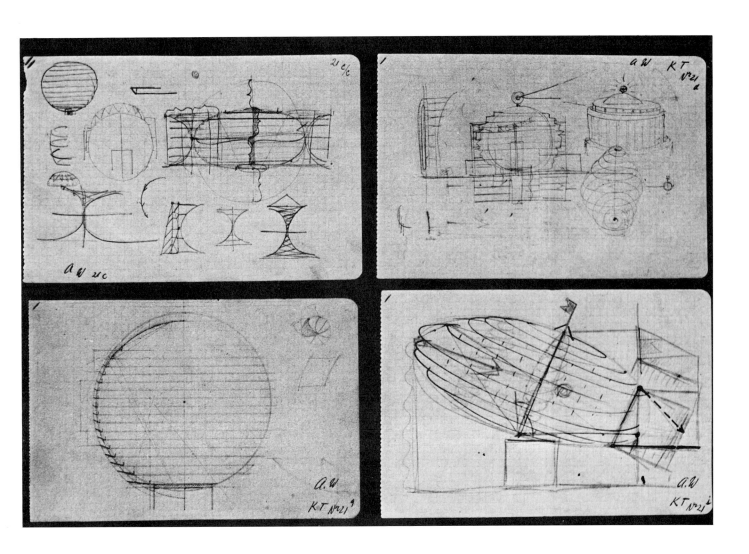

To stress the unreal I named it "House Fantasia." I do not remember having seen any architectural examples similar to my sketch by De Stijl in 1922.
I did not show it to Van Doesburg, in order to avoid being accused of romanticism.

119   Spherical Theater, different shapes   *(fig. 95b)*

Sketchbook page (also on verso), 1927
Pencil and colored pencil on graph paper, 5⅛ x 7⅝" (13 x 19.3 cm.)
Signed: "A.W." in ballpoint
Lent by Andrew Weininger

120   Spherical Theater, different shapes   *(fig. 95c)*

Sketchbook page (also on verso), 1927
Pencil and colored pencil on graph paper, 5⅛ x 7⅝" (13 x 19.3 cm.)
Signed: "A.W." in ballpoint
Lent by Andrew Weininger

121   Spherical Theater, precise drawing of seating tiers, section   *(fig. 95d)*

Sketchbook page (also on verso), 1927
Pencil and colored pencil on graph paper, 5⅛ x 7⅝" (13 x 19.3 cm.)
Signed: "A.W." in ballpoint
Lent by Andrew Weininger

122   Spherical Theater, tilted ellipsoid form   *(fig. 95e)*

Sketchbook page (also on verso), 1927
Colored pencil and ink on graph paper, 5⅛ x 7⅝" (13 x 19.3 cm.)
Signed: "A.W." in ballpoint
Lent by Andrew Weininger

To the Spherical Theater
At the Bauhaus "Raumgestaltung" (space-forming) was of prime importance. Schlemmer adopted the concept for our stage with the name "Raumbühne" (space-stage). In 1927 we demonstrated our new intentions with a performance, but were conscious of our limitations. I thought that ours was a conservative kind of stage, with the curtain dividing it from the auditorium.

How to solve the question of "Raumbühne?"
Near my home a travelling circus set up its tent, and the noisy gala premiere impressed me: the arena, the round row of seats, the high tent under which trapeze artists performed breathtakingly. In space! Was here not an answer? But the trained horse scenes, the wild animals, and the smells created doubts.
In my quest I now remembered the antique theaters, wherein mostly serious plays were performed. In history books I found descriptions and pictures. Drawing the rows of seats circular as in the circus, and using the half-spherical shape in place of the conical, would bring the far-away spectators nearer to the orchestra. In place of the tent, the "roof" could be a continuation of the hemispherical shape into a full sphere. It was a daring decision to let the rows continue further upward, as high as possible.
The gain was a surprise: interior space, giving all kinds of new possibilities and almost ideal viewing. In my sketches I contemplated other shapes, too; for instance, the ellipsoid. Although it was not realized, I was happy with my idea of a space-theater when it was first exhibited at the Magdeburger Theater Ausstellung in March 1927 *(fig. 95a)*.

Andrew Weininger

Williams, Amancio (Buenos Aires, 1913-)

Son of Argentina's most famous musical composer, Williams has been successively an engineer, aviator, and architect.

His studio in Buenos Aires has been not only the center for his practice and visionary projects but also is a school in which many young architects now prominent as professionals received their early training. Although his commissioned works are of great quality he is known primarily for his projects which have been published and exhibited internationally, including the House over the Brook at Mar del Plata. In 1947 Williams's projects were the theme of a special article that Le Corbusier wrote in a leading architectural magazine L'Homme et L'Architecture, Paris.

In 1968 Amancio Williams was selected to be the Argentine consultant architect to work with Walter Gropius on the planning and design of a new German Embassy in Buenos Aires. Since 1975 he has been working on a major research project entitled "The City that Humanity Needs" which is being carried forward in collaboration with colleagues in the University of Montevideo, Harvard University, and the University of Michigan, and which is expected to be published in the near future.

123 Hall for plastic spectacle and sound in space, section. (fig. 27)

Rendering, 1937-1953
Collage of gouache, ink, and cardboard on heavy cardboard, 27¼ x 39" (69 x 99 cm.)
Signed: "Amancio Williams, B.A., 1939-1942, 1943, 1953"
Lent by Amancio Williams

124 "Espectáculos Plásticos," Hall for plastic spectacle and sound in space, section (fig. 96)
Titled: "sala y espectáculo de plástica pura tres aparatos parecidos
    a los proyectores de planetarios realizan juegos de luces de
    extraordinaria diversidad de forma, color, y calidad. cada
    uno de estos proyectores puede moverse independientemente
    dentro de la sala." [88]
    "sala y espectáculo de plástica pura
    el triángulo es un piano o un prisme que se mueve dentro de
    la sala. una línea blanca describe un movimiento en
    contrapunto respecto al triángulo y línea se mueven en las
    tres dimensiones y pueden cambiar de color." [89]
125 "Espectáculos Plásticos," Hall for plastic spectacle and
sound in space, section
Titled: "sala y espectáculo de plástica pura una serie de lineas
    blancas describen movimientos en las tres dimensiones con
    ritmos determinados, sus colores pueden ser cambiantes
    la iluminación de la sala hará con los sistemas corrientes
    pero sobre todo con un nuevo sistema que permite iluminar en
    forma uniforme la atmósfera de la sala. en el color de esta
    lámina se ha querido dar una idea de uniformidad de dicha
    coloración
    espectáculos de este tipo formarán poco a poco directores de
    espectaculos plásticos e instrumentistas plásticos. los
    directores llegaran a dirigir espectáculos con partituras
    plásticas compuestas por creadores plásticos. [90]
Diagram with explanation, 1939-1953
Collage of paper, blue watercolor, and ink on paper, 38¾ x 26¾"
(98.5 x 58 cm.)
Signed: "Amancio Williams, B.A., 1939-1943, 1943, 1953"
Lent by Amancio Williams

This project was described by Gianni Rigoli in Zodiac 16 (1966) as follows: "The design of this huge mass of concrete in space, standing almost on one point and encircled by an aerial glass Saturn-like ring may arouse in the observer the question of what the reasons were to adopt this unprecedented form.

"The answer is simple: this form, structure in itself, is the architectural expression of a perfect technical solution. It is the outer part of a shell which is, inside, the closed space in which 3,500 to 6,500 can hear and see in the best conditions. It is a surface generated by the revolution of a curve around a central vertical axis, and this curve is the result of mathematical calculations for the perfect solution of acoustical problems. From the beginning of acoustics as a science, the problem in designing a hall was how to reinforce direct sound by its reflections, without echoes. A second problem was to get a quality called "the ideal reverberation time" as the scientist Sabine put it. He studied all the concert halls and theaters which had good acoustic conditions and found a formula relating volume, absorption and time. . . .

"Williams' aim was ambitious: to achieve the maximum balance of sound between the spectators by distributing all the reflecting surface so that the less direct sound one receives, the more reflected sound he gets. He was still working with the fan-shaped plan, but he considered not only the rear wall but the side walls and the ceiling. He pushed the fan-shaped plan to its utmost possibilities, to find that it was no longer good for a really complete solution. Side walls had to disappear and become one with the ceiling.

"Williams found a curve, the ideal reflecting profile which distributed reflections proportionally to the distance of the spectator from the focus. . . The proportionality works for any position of the focus. . . .

"Free of acoustical or visibility problems, the stage-manager can project his spectacle in the way he wants, be it on the central stage or in any place in the space. The action, or the dance, or the choruses can be performed in one or as many stages as wanted.

"The creator of pure plastic spectacles has almost no limit to his imagination. Form, color, light, movement are his raw materials; he can do anything with them. Electronic devices can organize and control every desired effect. The illumination of this hall is a challenge for every creator in this field. The immense curved surface is apt to receive any kind of projections; the space underneath can be lighted in the most fantastic way. One can imagine jets of colored light sprouting in a black atmosphere, like fireworks; another may think of luminous clouds of gas or steam; another will find how to give color and light to the air itself.

"In an age where physics and chemistry move in the realm of the miraculous, man needs a place where the newest possibilities provided by science can be used for the benefit of art. Williams' hall is that place."

96. *Williams, Hall for plastic spectacle.* No. 124.

Diagrams with explanations, 1939-1953
Collage of paper, blue watercolor, and ink on paper, 38¾ x 26¾"
(98.5 x 58 cm.)
Signed: "Amancio Williams, B.A., 1939-1942, 1943, 1953"
Lent by Amancio Williams

Wright, Frank Lloyd (Richland Center, Wisconsin, 1867—Phoenix, Arizona, 1959)

Frank Lloyd Wright was eighty-two years old when he designed the Auerbach house in 1949. his practice was flourishing in the midst of the boom that had begun in the late 1930s with the construction of the Kaufmann House, the Johnson Wax Administration Building, and the Jacobs House, the first Usonian. Two major buildings contemporary with the Auerbach project are the Unitarian Church in Shorewood Hills, Wisconsin, and the Guggenheim Museum. Community planning interested Wright throughout his career. In 1901 he proposed a "quadrangle block plan" for suburban houses, and in 1913 he entered a competition sponsored by the National Conference on City Planning for a suburban development. This project was a forerunner of the Broadacre City design of the early 1930s. Wright encouraged the application of his ideas in Broadacre City to the planning of communities of Usonian houses. The first of these cooperative developments, Usonia I, planned in 1939, was not realized, but in 1947 Wright prepared site plans for three communities that were built, two in Michigan, and Usonian Homes in Pleasantville, New York.

126 House for Mr. and Mrs. Erwin Auerbach, Usonia II, Mt. Pleasant, New York, plot plan *(fig. 97)*
127 House for Mr. and Mrs. Erwin Auerbach, Usonia II, Mt. Pleasant, New York, floor plan and perspective overview *(fig. 1)*
Rendering, 1949
Pencil and colored pencil on tracing paper, 35¾ x 37" (91 x 94 cm.), Scale: ¼" = 1' 0"
Unsigned
Lent by the Avery Architectural Library, Columbia University, gift of Philip I. Danzig

Though the Auerbach house represents a buildable project designed for a specific client, it must still be considered visionary, because in its context as a Usonion House it is charged with a conception greater than the solution of the problem of housing one particular family. Usonia, for Wright, was that society in which all things are organic. Broadacre City was to be the physical embodiment of that ideal, and the usonian houses and communities actually designed by Wright were attempts to realize the ideal in the all too unorganic United States. Thus, when Wright designed the site plan and a number of houses for the Rochdale cooperative development in Pleasantville, New York, referred to as Usonia II on the Auerbach house drawings, he spoke to members of the community about the virtues of Usonian life.

Low cost, an important element in Wright's definition of the Usonian house in the 1930s, ceased to be a distinguishing factor for him after World War II as he broadened the meaning of Usonian to include all his buildings. The Auerbach House, with its substantial foundatins and extensive use of fieldstone, would not have been inexpensive, but its compact, open plan generated by a module links it with those houses generally Usonian.

The mediium and style of the Auerbach drawings are typical of the work produced by Wright's studio, but the sensitive touch characteristic of his own drawings is absent. It is likely that these renderings were prepared by a member of the Taliesin Fellowship, a common practice in the 1940s and 1950s. Both drawings express the importance of siting in the design of a Usonian; the angular layout of the Auerbach plan (no. 127, fig. 1) corresponds to the angularity of the house itself, while the circular form of the plot of (no. 126, fig. 97) represents the fifty circular plots into which Wright had originally divided the Pleasantville holdings.
Richard Cleary

97. *Frank Lloyd Wright, Auerbach House.* No. 126.

Rendering, April 15, 1949
Pencil and colored pencil on tracing paper, 37 x 34½" (94 x 87.5
cm.), Scale: ⅛" = 1' 0"
Unsigned
Lent by Avery Architectural Library, Columbia University, gift of
Philip I. Danzig

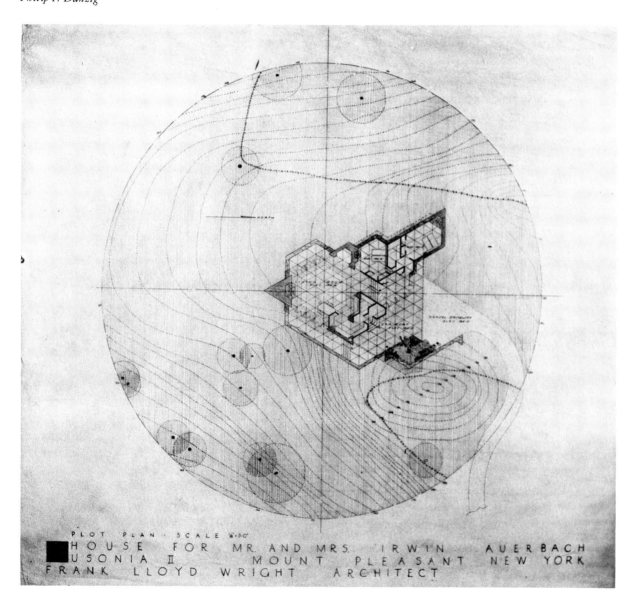

PLOT PLAN · SCALE ⅛"·1'0"
HOUSE   FOR   MR. AND MRS.   IRWIN   AUERBACH
USONIA II   MOUNT   PLEASANT   NEW YORK
FRANK   LLOYD   WRIGHT   ARCHITECT

Wright, Lloyd (Oak Park, 1890—Santa Monica, 1978)

Frank Lloyd Wright, Jr., known as Lloyd Wright, was the eldest of Frank Lloyd Wright's six children. In 1909 he interrupted his first year at the University of Wisconsin to help his father prepare the Wasmuth portfolio in Italy, but in the fall of 1910 he returned to the university for another year of study.
Lloyd Wright found work in 1911 as a draftsman-delineator with the landscape architects Olmsted and Olmsted. His job took him to California where in 1912 he joined the office of Irving J. Gill. In 1916-17 he headed Paramount's set design department.
From 1919 to 1927 Lloyd Wright worked with his father on projects in California and Arizona and began to build an independent practice as a landscape designer and as an architect. He also designed stage sets (1922-25) and two acoustical shells (1924-25, 1928) for the Hollywood Bowl Association.
Large-scale planning projects interested Lloyd Wright throughout his career. he published a "City of the Future" and a scheme for central Los Angeles during 1925-26, co-designed two Los Angeles housing projects between 1939-42, and prepared a visionary plan for Los Angeles County in the early 1960s. Though Lloyd Wright's houses received little attention outside of California, he achieved national recognition with the Wayfarer's Chapel in Palos Verdes after World War II.

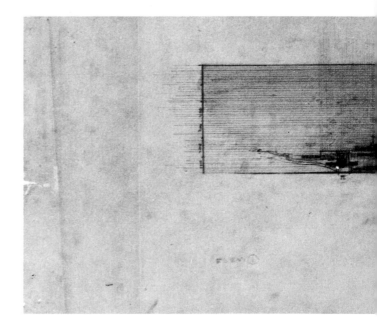

128   Civic Center Project, perspective elevation   *(fig. 98)*

129   Civic Center Project, section   *(fig. 18)*

Rendering for newspaper, 1925
Ink on tracing paper, 4⅛ x 10⅛" (10.5 x 26 cm.)
Unsigned
Lent by Eric Lloyd Wright

Between 1920 and 1925 the population of Los Angeles nearly doubled, and the city found itself faced with the problem of providing services for over one million people and a rapidly increasing number of motor vehicles. By 1925 a plan had been prepared for a county-wide transportation network radiating from a civic center designed by the Allied Architects Association of Los Angeles, a consortium of the city's leading architectural firms. The Allied Architects effectively kept smaller firms from participating in the

98.   *Lloyd Wright, Civic Center Project.* No. 128.

Rendering, 1925
Pencil with tempera on tracing paper, 8⅛ x 32¾" (22.8 x 83.2 cm.)
Unsigned
Scale on drawing
Lent by Eric Lloyd Wright

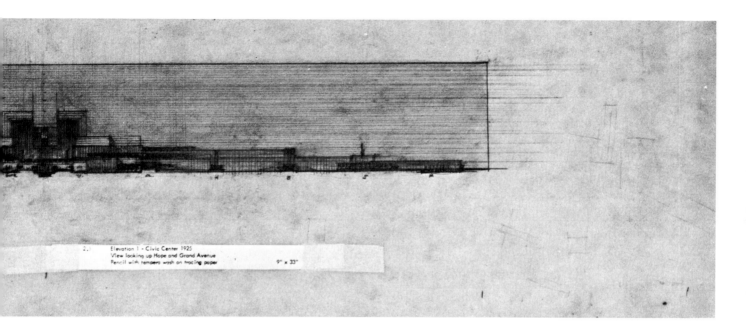

Elevation 1 - Civic Center 1925
View looking up Hope and Grand Avenue
Pencil with tempera wash on tracing paper   9" x 33"

project, and Lloyd Wright's plan, published in the *Los Angeles Times* of August 30, 1925, offered an alternative proposal. Lloyd Wright arranged his buildings along a cruciform plan similar to that governing the Allied Architects' classical project, but where they had envisioned a place of repose, Lloyd Wright created one of action that brings to mind futurist schemes. Pedestrians, automobiles, and trains hurry along multi-level corridors. Aircraft land on a precariously sited airstrip, and dirigibles hover above. Underground there were to have been parking garages and tunnels linking the buildings which were to have housed governmental offices and museums. A multi-level boulevard along the main axis was to have connected the civic center with a large exposition park, and other boulevards were to have fed a system of parkways leading to a ring highway around the city.

Lloyd Wright prepared the section of the civic center *(fig. 18)* for newspaper reproduction, using strong areas of light and dark to clearly define the essential forms. The more delicately rendered color view *(fig. 98)* appears to have been a study for the massing of the entire complex. The major buildings increase in height over the length of the main axis creating the effect of a Mayan stepped pyramid, but their individual forms have more of an Art Deco feeling. Though Lloyd Wright claimed his proposal would be economical to realize, its monumental scale was perhaps better suited to the economics of a Hollywood spectacular than to the budget of a city.

130   1,000-foot-high building, "City of the Future," overviews, sections, calculations   *(fig. 19)*

Perspective sketches, 1926
Pencil on tracing paper, 15¾ x 30⅞" (40 x 78.3 cm.)
Unsigned
Lent by Eric Lloyd Wright

Readers of the *Los Angeles Examiner* opening their papers on November 26, 1926, found themselves looking at Lloyd Wright's dramatic rendering for a "City of the Future" developed from the studies on the sheet shown here. Lloyd Wright's project, a potpourri of some of the most recent ideas for skyscrapers, proposed a city of reinforced-concrete towers, 1,000' high, faced with gleaming surfaces of bronze and glass, and containing housing, industry, and entertainment facilities for 150,000 people. Each tower would be

surrounded by farms and parkland and linked to the other towers by high-speed transportation corridors.

The towers were to be built on slabs floating on reservoirs of liquid mud intended to cushion the shock of an earthquake. Lloyd Wright adopted this system from that used on a much smaller scale by his father for the Imperial Hotel in Tokyo (1915-22). The "City of the Future's" superstructure recalls Frank Lloyd Wright's projects for the Press Building in San Francisco (1912) and the National Life Insurance Company Skyscraper in Chicago (1924), but Lloyd Wright's proposal is on a scale that is not typical of Frank Lloyd Wright's work at this time.

Lloyd Wright's scheme is an early example of a tall building equipped with a rooftop airport. The concept was central to his vision. Most of the small perspective sketches illustrate flocks of biplanes swarming around the towers which in one instance he has labeled "Rookery" (see notation at right).

131   Study for Los Angeles County Regional Urban Plan, site plan and section   *(fig. 51)*

Rendering, 1964
Colored pencil on tracing paper, 29¼ x 37⅞" (74.2 x 96.2 cm.)
Scale: 1½" = 1 mile
Signed: "LLOYD WRIGHT ARCHITECT 18 JANUARY 1964"

"It became apparent to me that the great star of this city was not *estancias;* they were not the focal point, but the Pacific Ocean front . . . I have coordinated highways and waterways to create marinas, great floating cities—a magnificent forefront for the city."[91]

From 1962 to 1965 Lloyd Wright worked on his plan to open Los Angeles to the the Pacific Ocean. The city's refuse was to be used to create a causeway along the coast, and a grand canal was to link the ocean with a new civic center. Traffic would move along park-lined highways, parking was to be underground, and large buildings were to be erected above the transportation arteries.

Lloyd Wright hoped his plan would act as a catalyst for the discussion of problems he felt were unresolved in official plans. Lloyd Wright's drawings share medium and technique with the work produced by his father's studio, and the buildings he rendered resemble either his own Mayan-Art Deco projects of the 1920s or the angular structures Frank

Lloyd Wright designed in the 1950s. The ample green spaces in Lloyd Wright's plan make a sharp contrast to the reality of the urban sprawl of modern Los Angeles.

Richard Cleary

NOTES

1. For instance, the Committee for the Preservation of Architectural Records, Inc., 15 Gramercy Park South, New York City.
2. Malcolmson, R., *Visionary Projects for Buildings and Cities,* Catalogue, 1974, p. vi.
3. Dictionaries do not help. We employ the term "visionary" to mean visionary concepts—not just visionary persons—a usage that does not yet appear in standard dictionaries.
4. Inge, W.R., *Christian Mysticism,* 1897, I, p. 14.
5. Opening statement in his *Internationale Neue Baukunst,* Stuttgart, 1927.
6. *Progressive Architecture,* CXXIII, September 1965, p. 68.
7. Sir Walter Scott commented, "It becomes almost in vain to argue with the visionary against the reality of his dream," in *Letters on Demonology and Witchcraft,* 1830, I, p. 6.
8. *The Architect and Contract Reporter* (*Architect and Building News,* LXXX, London), 25 September 1908, pp. 196-97, and 6 November 1908, p. 303.
9. Japan Architect, XLVI (January-February, 1971), p. 26.
10. "Buildings like Mountains" has appeared under several titles. It was first shown in 1925 at the Anderson Galleries, New York, as "Similarities of these masses to mountainous masses," one of a group of futuristic illustrations based on the zoning envelope studies. In the January 1926 issue of *Baukunst,* it was entitled "Similarity of 'zoned' masses to mountainous masses," but it received by far its widest exposure when it was reproduced as the frontispiece of *The Metropolis of Tomorrow* (1929), entitled "Buildings like Mountains."
11. "Architectural Rendering," *Encyclopaedia Britannica,* 1936, XIX, pp. 147 and 148.
12. *Ibid.,* p. 149.
13. *Ibid.,* p. 143.
14. Ulrich Conrads and Hans G. Sperlich, *The Architecture of Fantasy,* translated, edited, and expanded by Christiane Crasemann Collins and George R. Collins, New York, 1962, p. 149. This is the only book which contains an English translation of some of Finsterlin's writings.
15. *Ibid.,* p. 143.
16. One version was published in Dennis Sharp, *Modern Architecture and Expressionism,* New York, 1966, p. 104, and in F. Borsi and G. K. König, *Architettura dell'Espressionismo,* Genoa, 1967, p. 290, fig. 126; a slightly different version appeared in Wolfgang Pehnt, *Expressionist Architecture,* New York/Washington, 1973, p. 93, fig. 207.
17. "Cathedral" was also illustrated in Sharp and in Borsi and König, as well as in Franco Borsi, *Hermann Finsterlin,* Florence, 1968, p. 186, pl. 34, and in *Wendingen,* No. 3, 6th series; the illustrations vary in very minor details.
18. During an interview with Finsterlin in the summer of 1964.
19. A 1932 date is claimed in Borsi's *Hermann Finsterlin,* and 1933 is listed as the year in which he lectured at the Bauhaus in *Die Gläserne Kette—Visionäre Architekturen aus dem Kreis um Bruno Taut 1919-1920,* exhibition catalogue, Museum Leverkusen, Schloss Morsbroich and Akademie der Künste Berlin, 1963, p. 118.
20. This is verified by Meyer himself in a letter written in 1930 on the occasion of his dismissal from the Bauhaus. See Hans Wingler, *The Bauhaus,* translated by Basil Gilbert and Wolfgang Jabs, Cambridge, Mass., 1969, p. 164.
21. Conrads and Sperlich, op. cit., p. 166, note 80.
22. *Ibid.,* p. 149.
23. *Architectural Design,* XLII, December 1972, p. 747.
24. Marks, Robert, *The Dymaxion World of Buckminster Fuller,* 1960, pp. 70-79.

25. Conversation with Medard Gabel, his archivist, on 23 September 1978, communicated to us by the latter.
26. Meyer, June, "Instant Slum Clearance," *Esquire,* April 1965, pp. 108-11.
27. Piscator's productions, which tried to destroy the illusion of naturalistic sets, anticipated similar stagings by Brecht. Though Piscator regarded most prewar theater as much too bourgeois, his innovations, were, nevertheless, influenced by Edward Gordon Craig's architectonic stark sets and by Max Reinhardt's use of lighting. Piscator had produced plays in Reinhardt's Grosses Schauspielhaus, which had been designed by Hans Poelzig in 1918-19, and containing a proscenium stage (Erwin Piscator, *Das Politische Theater,* reedited by Felix Gasbarre, Hamburg, Rowohlt, 1963).
28. The plan of the Total Theater bears a faint resemblance to Rudolf Steiner's first Goetheanum of 1913-20.
29. *The Theater of the Bauhaus,* edited and with an introduction by Walter Gropius, translated by Arthur S. Wensinger, Middletown, Wesleyan University Press, 1961. This was originally published in 1925 as volume 4 of the Bauhaus books.
30. James Marston Fitch, *Walter Gropius,* New York, Braziller, 1960, p. 23.
31. Hans M. Wingler, *The Bauhaus,* translated by Wolfgang Jabs and Basil Gilbert, edited by Joseph Stein, Cambridge, Mass., MIT Press, 1969, p. 419.
32. *Ibid.,* p. 58.
33. Although in 1927 Piscator was negotiating for a site in Berlin for the Total Theater, it was never executed because of the lack of funds (see Maria Ley-Piscator, *The Piscator Experiment—The Political Theater,* New York, Heineman, 1967, p. 83).
34. The flying-colony's overhead propeller mechanism hearkens back in principle to the one presented in Leonardo's famous drawing of a flying machine. See his notebook, Ms B. 83v., in the Library of the Institut de France, and published, with other Leonardo manuscripts, by Ravaisson Mollien, Paris, 1881-91.
35. Hablik included the flying settlement with some slight modifications in his 1925 folio, "Cyklus Architektur."
36. In the settlement as in the earlier "colony" there is evident a synthesis of elements inspired by both nature and the machine that is conveyed on the one hand by the airship's intricately-faceted crystalline core, and on the other by the taut enveloping lines of the drum and the tensile system of wires and props. Through the aphoristic statement placed on the drawing's larger backing sheet, Hablik presented his belief that the flying settlement would have been an integral part of the larger universal order: "Technical things are never impossible in-so-far as they are constructed in accord with natural laws. Also at one time natural laws were utopias." Hablik was seizing upon a theme, the pervasiveness and ultimate perfection of the laws of nature, that is dominant in nineteenth-century thought and is exemplified by the writings of Goethe and Schopenhauer. For parallels between natural and mechanistic systems, however, Hablik might have been inspired by Maurice Maeterlinck's *L'Intelligence des Fleurs* (original French edition and German edition, 1907) wherein the question is raised: "When shall we succeed in building a parachute or a flying-machine as rigid, as light, as subtle and as safe as that of the Dandelion?"
37. Elaborations upon this theme are contained in Bruno Taut's *Alpine Architektur,* Hagen i W., 1919, *Die Stadtkrone,* Jena, 1919, and *Die Auflösung der Städte,* Hagen i W., 1920.
38. Hablik included the image of the "Mountain-Cathedral" in his 1925 folio "Cyklus Architektur."

39. Hablik discussed his design methodology in "Die freitragende Kuppel und ihre Variabilität, unter Berücksichtigung verschiedener Materialien und Verwendungsmöglichkeiten," *Frühlicht*, v. 3 (Spring, 1922), pp. 94-98. Drawing border contains Platonic/Vitruvian "doubling the square" diagram.

40. Two towers similar to the one here appear in Hablik's "Cyklus Architektur" folio, where he described them as constructions in the Grand Canyon.

41. This drawing was created specifically to illustrate the essay, "Die Dome," which Hablik contributed in 1923 to the annual, *Schöpfung, Beiträge zu einer Weltgeschichte religiöser Kunst*.

42. Two such domical structures appear in Hablik's "Cyklus Architektur" folio.

43. In his essay of 1923, Hablik elaborated upon the possibility that one day many cathedrals could stand as testaments to world unity.

44. Banham, R., *Megastructure: Urban Futures of the Recent Past*, New York, 1976, p. 21.

45. URTEC, Urbanists and Architects Team, a cooperative of designers and engineers formed by Kenzo Tange in 1961 on the model of TAC (The Architects' Collaborative).

46. From a poster used for an exhibition of Isozaki's work in Kyushu in 1976. Reproduced and translated in *Japan Architect* #247 (Oct.-Nov., 1977), pp. 20-21.

47. Flier, Atlas Cement, subsidiary of U.S. Steel, [1957], pp.1-2.

48. Kiesler, *Inside the Endless House, Art, People and Architecture. A Journal*, 1960, pp. 408-9, quoting "Li."

49. *Ibid.*, p. 104.

50. *Ibid.*, p. 173.

51. *Ibid.*, p. 569.

52. *Ibid.*, p. 308.

53. Kiesler, Foreword to Catalogue, *International Theatre Exposition*, New York, 1926.

54. Kiesler, quoting Louis Kahn, *Inside the Endless House*, p. 513.

55. Kiesler, *Chicago Tribune*, 1920.

56. In *Kokusai Kenchiku*, February 1959.

57. K. Kikutake in *Idem*, January 1959.

58. *The Craftsman*, April 1904, p. 6.

59. For instance, in Inigo Triggs, *Town Planning Past and Present*, London, 1909.

60. *The Craftsman*, April 1904, pp. 3 ff.

61. Le Corbusier, *When the Cathedrals Were White*, New York, 1964, pp. 194-95.

62. *Four Great Makers of Modern Architecture: Gropius, Le Corbusier, Mies van der Rohe, Wright*, Symposium, Columbia University, 1961, New York City, 1970, p. 165.

63. *Ibid.*, pp. 166-67.

64. *Ibid.*, pp. 169-70.

65. Extracts from 1969 taped interviews of Robert Le Ricolais by Peter McCleary and *VIA 2* editors. Published as "Interviews with Robert Le Ricolais 'Things Themselves are Lying and so are their Images,'" *VIA* Vol. 2 (1973), publication of the Graduate School of Fine Arts, University of Pennsylvania.

66. Compare the hexagonal city plan of Charles R. Lamb *(fig. 3)*.

67. "My own Contribution to the Development of Contemporary Architecture," typescript in Avery Architectural Library, Columbia University, New York City, p. 5.

68. Oskar Beyer, ed., *Letters of an Architect*, 1967, p. 43.

69. *Magazine of Art*, December 1945, pp. 307-08.

70. Beyer, op. cit., p. 40.

71. Philip C. Johnson, *Mies van der Rohe*, Museum of Modern Art, New York, 1953, p. 187. In other contemporary studies Mies used photomontage, in which he was apparently an innovator for architectural drawings (R. Malcolmson, in *Hogar y Arquitectura*, Madrid, Nos. 108-09, 1973, p. 39.)

72. *Shelter: T. Square*, March 1938, p. 23, seems to indicate that no. 79 was drawn in 1923; no. 80 and no. 81 were published in his *Wie baut Amerika* of 1927. Neutra's widow tells us that Addison Hehr was his student and not his collaborator in these drawings (as *Shelter* implies), but only on the general project.

73. *Idem*, p. 33.

74. Roland, C., *Frei Otto: Tension Structures*, New York, 1970, pp. 150-51.

75. Idem.

76. *Newsweek*, 16 August 1976, p. 79.

77. Soleri, P., *Sketchbooks*, December 1962, p. 380.

78. Tyng, A.G., *Simultaneous Randomness and Order: The Fibonacci-Divine Proportion as a Universal Forming Principle*," Ph.D. dissertation, University Microfilms International, Ann Arbor, Mich., London, 1975.

79. Granit, R., *Receptors and Sensory Perception*, New Haven, 1955.

80. Wittkower, R., "The Changing Concept of Proportion," *Daedalus*, 1961, p. 211.

81. Tyng, A.G., *op. cit.*, pp. 19-20.

82. Tyng, A.G., "Geometric Extensions of Consciousness," *Zodiac* 19.

83. Wachsmann, K., *The Turning Point of Building; Structure and Design*, New York, 1961, pp. 170-172.

84. *Ibid.*, p. 194. This two-part drawing has always been reproduced by flipping it vertically to double it, and printing it in black on white.

85. 'room' is called Suitaloon.

86. This would be believable, were it not for the fact that house, car, and suit each have their own styling lore, to evoke differing fantasies (car: speed, modern, rounded corners, sex, etc.; house: trad, colonial, square corners).

87. 'car' is called a "cushicle," abbreviation of air cushion vehicle.

88. "Room [space] and performance of pure plasticity. Three apparatuses like projectors of planetariums make light-play of extraordinary diversity of form, color, and quality. Each of these projectors can be moved independently in the room."

89. "Room [space] and performance of pure plasticity. The triangle is a piano or a prism which moves within the room. A white line indicates a movement in counterpoint with respect to the triangle and lines that move in three dimensions and can change color."

90. "Room [space] and performance of pure plasticity. A series of white lines indicates movements in three dimensions with specific rhythms. Their colors can be changed. The illumination of the rooms will be done with available systems, but especially with a new system that allows illumination of the atmosphere of the rooms in consistent form. In the color of these sheets we have wished to give an idea of uniformity of the colors. Spectacles of this type will produce little by little conductors of plastic spectacles and plastic instruments. The conductors will succeed in directing spectacles with plastic scores composed by plastic creators."

91. Interview with Esther McCoy, "Lloyd Wright," in *Arts & Architecture*, LXXXIII, October 1966, p. 24.

Photographic Credits

Where no credit is listed, the photographic print was supplied by the lender listed. Numbers refer to figure numbers.